LINUS JONKMAN

INTROVERT
THE FRIENDLY TAKEOVER

Printed in the United States of America
First Printing, 2016
ISBN-13: 978-9198327618 (National library of Sweden)

Egonaut Consulting AB
Litografigatan 3
262 63 Engelholm
Sweden

www.linusjonkman.com

Credits
Author: Linus Jonkman
Translation (to English): Jan Salomonsson
Publisher: Anders Sjöqvist
Editor: Andreas Lundberg
Cover: Pär Wickholm

For Smilla and Ludvig

The wind howls, but the mountain remains still
Japanese proverb

Table of Contents

It's Springtime for Introverts.. 9

Beyond the Cork Tree – What Does "Introvert" Mean?.......15

Coming out of the Social Closet...23

Time Travel to an Unexpected Destination...............................35

The Introvert and Extravert Psyches...47

Can You Make Yourself More Extraverted
   (and Would You Want to)? 71

Do Extraverts Have the Gift of the Gab?....................................85

Meaningful Encounters 99

Is introversion a disadvantage?..115

Solitude vs. Loneliness 129

How Introverts and Extraverts Relate to Each Other 135

The Power of Introversion...159

An Uplifting Upbringing...181

Introverts at work...193

What's the Best Working Environment,
   and the Best Kind of Leadership? 209

Finding Your Cork Tree...233

Test – Are you Stuck in a Closet?..241

The Cocktail Version – Extraversion vs. Introversion 255

Sources 259

It's Springtime for Introverts

The opening gala was an orgy of self-promotion. The place was swarming with young fashionistas in stripy sweaters, thick-rimmed glasses and fedoras. Middle-aged media types with bright red indoor tans, who were dressed to look twenty years younger than they really were, rubbed up against cheek kissing, rosé sipping, careerists. The hip factor was off the charts. Somebody skateboarded through the room. Waitresses in stilettos zipped around among all the five-day stubbles and ironic T-shirts, handing out free drinks. Wherever I looked, people were trying to make new connections. Young entrepreneurs were on the hunt for eye contact and business cards. Established businesses were vying for my attention, eager to tell me about their service offerings. The moment I so much as looked at somebody, they would approach me and begin a conversation. Wherever I turned, I saw people in full-blown networking mode. My collar felt tight. I felt like a thousand eyes were judging my every move. This busy place had no nooks and crannies, just bright polished epoxy flooring. After an hour of this, my shirt was soaked through with sweat, and I smelled like ammonia. I felt like I'd just run a marathon.

When I emerged into the cool air of this late summer evening, a deep sigh of relief passed through me. I could breathe again. My reaction surprised me, as did the relief I felt. That evening, I mulled over my behavior. Before sleep overcame me, I realized the undeniable fact I had been struggling to keep from myself: I'm an introvert.

"Is this the new lactose intolerant?" a sarcastic friend asked when I told him of my discovery. First, I laughed. But my laughter soon rang false, when I realized that there actually were a number of similarities.

The word *introvert* has made its way onto more and more headlines of late. It's often used to describe people who are withdrawn, reticent, and absent-minded.

The problem with lactose intolerance was that hardly anybody looked for signs that they suffered from it before it became widely publicized. Everybody in the West was convinced that milk was great for you. It made kids grow up strong, and was full of nutrients. Suddenly, lactose intolerance was the latest buzzword, and everybody started trying to figure out if they were among the millions of people who turned out to be afflicted. Right now, I think the introversion trend has a lot in common with that phenomenon. We're not looking for signs that we're introverts, for the simple reason that we're convinced that we're extraverts, i.e., outgoing, because that happens to be the norm in our society.

But it's wrong to call it a buzzword. The concept of introversion is one of the oldest terms in psychology, coined almost a century ago by Carl Jung. It's been referred to as the *Mother of all Personality Traits*, and is thought to be a dominant aspect of the behavior of all placental mammals.

Here's a question for you to consider:

> *Would you rather:*
>
> *A – spend every moment alone for two whole weeks, or*
>
> *B – have people you know around you every moment for two whole weeks?*

If your response is A, you're likely to be more of an introvert (i.e., predominantly reflective and withdrawn). If your response is B, you're probably an extravert (i.e., sociable and outgoing). If you can't make up your mind, perhaps you're an ambivert (i.e., a little bit of both). These personality traits entail a number of amazing talents that were unknown to us until quite recently.

Hi, my name is Linus, and I'm an introvert. Some of the most meaningful events in my life never even happened. The most valuable things in my life are the ones that happen inside my own skull. My imagination, various stories, and the things I'm thinking about are sources of refuge for me in this age of self-promotion, constant networking and group assignments. We live in a time when books, as well as all other things, are judged by their covers more often than not.

Outgoing people attract attention to themselves through their own social energy. They make sure to be heard and seen. When somebody confidently describes himself as *outgoing* in a job interview, it's taken as a positive. We assume that the term somehow entails social competence, even though it really doesn't. Being outgoing simply means that you have a social *need*, which is something else entirely. There are outgoing people who are incapable of leaving any room for others to speak during meetings, and who go on and on about their own interests without paying any attention to anybody else. At the same time, some people who are quite withdrawn are excellent listeners, and very good at relating to other people. Social competence isn't the exclusive domain of one or the other side of this spectrum.

Introverts and extraverts operate on different levels: extraverts rule the bar, and introverts rule the mind.

Labels

Where does all the new terminology that keeps appearing in the media week after week come from? Introversion seems to be a big deal right now. HSP is a fairly popular term as well. It might sound like some kind of brake system, but HSP is actually an acronym for *Highly Sensitive Person*, and the personality type it refers to has begun to be discussed in the news. Another common term is *Millennials*, which denotes a group of people who were born in the 1980s and 1990s. We seem to like to generalize and categorize people. Is this always a bad thing, or can it actually be helpful?

I'm privileged enough to have a very varied bunch of people in my life, whose personalities range across the entire scale. This helps me understand and relate to both extraversion and introversion. The content of this book mainly focuses on people like myself, i.e., introverts. There's not much point in writing a book for extraverts, seeing as they're all too busy kitesurfing, doing Zumba, and sipping lattes to read books. A version for extraverts would probably have to be a picture book. I hope to be able to encourage others to come out of their extraverted closets. I think there are a lot of people who are introverts deep down, but simply don't believe or admit that they are, even to themselves.

The introverted personality is thought to account for just over a quarter of the global population. We're a minority in the regular population, but a majority in the gifted population. I realize that this statement might ruffle some feathers. I'll explain what I mean in greater detail later on in this book.

One of my closest friends surprised me the other day. After reading an article about the introverted personality, he told me that he felt like he'd finally found his way home. You might be surprised to learn that he's an experienced musician, who has toured the world and met fans in the thousands. He's used to being the center of attention in a large crowd.

"Linus, I have to confess to something. I've always felt like there was something wrong with me. Sometimes, at release parties, I've hidden in the bathroom, because I felt exhausted and overwhelmed by it all. Then, I read that article, and I realized that I'm not crazy, I'm an introvert."

When I was doing my research for this book, I noticed how terribly misunderstood the whole concept of introversion seems to be. The word "extravert" is commonly used in want ads, while "introvert" seems to have been reserved for articles about charming types like Jeffrey Dahmer.

Fortunately, after these last few years of publicity, this has begun to change. One of the signs I've seen of this change was a résumé that landed on my desk the other week. In it, the applicant had described himself as an "Introvert (even before it was trendy)"

I stumbled over an old newspaper article about introversion, which concluded that the introverts inhabit limited worlds, because they're mainly interested in themselves. Nothing could be further from the truth. An introvert's world is boundless in scope.

After reading a fair amount on this topic, I've noticed an alarming tendency. In her book *Quiet*, Susan Cain tells the story of an introverted college professor who they would always find in the bathroom before his lectures. He'd be stuck in front of the mirror with his forehead wet with sweat, struggling to summon the strength to enter the lecture hall. A journalist for The Times writes in his blog about how he often sneaks into the bathroom at cocktail parties, to recharge his batteries. I myself often use the bathroom to get a moment of silence before I walk on stage. This makes me a little concerned.

I don't really want to be representing a personality type whose main claim to fame is a propensity to occupy bathrooms. That's why I've decided to spread the word about all of the fascinating aspects of the terms introversion and extraversion. What we're talking about here are two aspects that we all possess to some degree.

We live in an age when we're expected to be outgoing, outspoken, and eager to make new connections. Many of us end up fighting our own nature in order to fulfill society's expectations that we be outgoing and spontaneous. I'd like to help people who've lost touch with their own introverted aspect. After the final chapter of this book, I've included a test that you can take to determine where you belong on this scale. This is the dawning of a reevaluation of the personalities that are prone to thinking a lot, and speaking a lot less; a friendly takeover of a word that has been given a pretty raw deal.

Beyond the Cork Tree –
What Does "Introvert" Mean?

"Now, Ferdinand, why don't you play with all the other little bulls and butt your head?"

Even though his mother is understanding, she delivers these words with a hint of compassion. I've always sympathized with the peaceful bull in Disney's cartoon. Ferdinand grows up to be a friendly giant, with no interest in anything but spending his time under the cork tree. The men in the funny hats drag him out into the world. They try to make Ferdinand act in accordance with the expectations of others. To me, this story is an accurate representation of the experiences of an introvert. Ferdinand is an anomaly in the eyes of the world: somebody who ought to get off his butt and achieve something.

Are you a social butterfly? Do you move through groups of people with ease, and can you speak to pretty much anybody? Are you constantly thirsting for new acquaintances, and curious about the people around you? Is connecting with people on a social level something you simply can't get enough of? Perhaps you have a brother who gets caught up in his hobbies, or maybe your dad is the strong silent type? Perhaps you're having trouble understanding your significant other's need for alone time? Then, you're probably not an introvert.

Introverts are those of us who can forget why we're on our way to the next room before we even get there. We're more consumed by our own inner thoughts than by the voices of the people around us in the coffee room. We're the ones who struggle with phone-o-phobia, and find meeting new people an exhausting ordeal. Maybe you're one of us? Maybe you've simply forgotten this fact, living as you do in a world dominated by extraverted ideals, which insist that we be outgoing and not shy away from the spotlight.

What exactly is an introvert? There's no shortage of stereotypes regarding this. According to people I know, the following all signify introversion:

- ✓ People with bowl cuts
- ✓ Napoleon Dynamite types
- ✓ People who'd rather stay at home knitting sweaters with cats on them than hang out
- ✓ People who watch the commentary track on Star Trek DVD's
- ✓ A musician who plays with his back to the audience

There are plenty of stereotypes regarding extraverts, too:

- ✓ A resting pulse of 200 beats per minute
- ✓ Howard Stern
- ✓ The kind of people who audition for *Big brother* and have "tramp stamp" tattoos
- ✓ People who can't stop talking about their favorite topic: themselves
- ✓ People who don't think twice about discussing their STD test results on the phone while riding a packed commuter train

Let's leave our preconceived notions behind, and approach this from a psychological perspective. The core of the issue is basically how you respond to the following question: *Do you recharge your energy by interacting with other people, or by thinking things over in solitude?*

However, there are far more aspects to introversion than this. It affects our strengths, talents, relationships, and health, as well as a large number of other facets of our lives. Lately, I've become convinced that the degree to which we're introverted or extraverted is the most defining characteristic of our personalities.

Shy? Asocial? Arrogant? No, introverted

Introversion is mainly evident in the fact that you're energized by the thoughts you have when you're alone. This doesn't mean you have to be the only person in the room, just that you need to do something that doesn't involve any social interaction. Spending time with other people, especially in large groups, drains you of energy, and makes you feel physically exhausted after a while. When your batteries run out, you'll be irritable, restless, and uncomfortable. Conversing with smaller groups of people, who give each other plenty of space to take part, and who are usually other introverts, is much less exhausting.

This isn't a lifestyle, it's not something you've chosen. It's not some fashion trend or subculture. Being introverted is the result of biological hardwiring; it's in your DNA. Studies performed on identical twins have shown beyond any doubt that it's a matter of nature, not nurture. This personality trait should really be thought of as a need. Introversion is the need for solitude.

Oh, well. What's a royal ball?

The opposite of introversion is extraversion. An extravert is energized by conversing with other people. Crowds and conversations are battery chargers for extraverts. To put it in simple terms: introverts need solitude, extraverts need company. Even though both types might appreciate company equally, it can get to be too much of a good thing for the introvert. A good example of this is what happens when my wife Hanna and I go to parties. On the way there, we're both in high spirits, listening to loud music, and talking the whole time. On the way home, Hanna does all the talking, and I sit in silence. My batteries are drained, but she's all full of new impressions to share.

17

Being an introvert involves confronting a fundamental problem: contemporary Western society idealizes social virtues. Introverts can easily come across as unambitious, shy, or arrogant, and this tends to hinder them at times. For instance, how many job listings have you seen that say they're looking for an introvert? But there's a light at the end of the tunnel. The sudden renaissance of behavioral science and psychology has provided some room for reconsideration. What used to be dusty old science has become part of popular culture. People from all walks of life have begun to ponder what their true personalities are. When they first hear the words extravert and introvert, many people try to decide which category they belong to. One of my friends read the draft of this book, and told me that he suffered something of an identity crisis when he reached the final page. Why does this happen? How can the most defining feature of our personalities be so unknown to us? Probably because somebody reshaped it for us.

This somebody I'm referring to is our society and its zeitgeist. We live in an age where extraversion seems to have become an unquestionable norm. Many of the rules we live by are really only designed to suit the extraverted segments of the population. Here are some extravert truths:

- ✓ Positive thinking is the key to success.
- ✓ You get the best results by working in groups.
- ✓ Somebody who keeps their office door closed is depressed.
- ✓ Children need constant physical activity.
- ✓ Being on your own is less fun than having company.
- ✓ Efficient people multi-task.

Assumptions like these are based on our extraverted societal norms.

However, things weren't always this way. It used to be that the ideal was for people to be introverts. Old sayings such as "silence is golden" are relics of this era. It was considered rude to speak about yourself, or use the word me. The man of few words, as exemplified by John Wayne, remained the ideal until the 1960s.

Longitudinal studies have been performed to investigate the things that mothers have thought important to teach their children. In the 1940s, *discipline* and *loyalty* were generally considered the finest of virtues. After this, the 1960s followed, with all of the dizzying change brought about by trailblazers like Martin Luther King, Rosa Parks, and John F Kennedy. Youth culture was born. Before the 1950s, the concept of a teenager was unheard of; the world was simply populated by children and adults. And it suddenly got a whole lot noisier when the Rolling Stones, the Beatles, and Elvis encouraged us all to be ourselves. Iggy, Ziggy, and Twiggy all contributed to shaping an era where each individual became the center of his or her own universe. Now, everybody was expected to communicate their appearance, sexuality, and opinions loudly whenever the opportunity arose. This previously reserved culture, where everybody thought of the collective, the family, or society first, was changing. Instead, we were beginning to think like individuals, and focus on ourselves and our own needs. The older, more restrained role models and authority figures, who had been the pillars of our society, were replaced by youth and the individual, which would come to take center-stage in the new society that was emerging.

A newly awakened generation was suddenly focusing their attention on their egos, and on their own paths to happiness. The generations which had preceded it had hardly given the questions of whether or not they were happy or doing fulfilling work any thought. Today, when asked about the most important thing to teach your children, mothers answer that "children need to learn to stand up for themselves and their opinions". Another common idea is that "they should follow their inner voice, and have the courage to aim for the stars". These are extraverted ideals. They celebrate the social human being. In the old world of collective thought, before the 1950s, the most important thing was fitting in. You needed to earn your place and give back to society. In those days, the quiet workhorse was the hero.

Planet Introvert?

This field of study was first opened up for inquiry 2,500 years ago. A Greek philosopher named Hippocrates, was walking along the beach, deep in thought. He scribbled his ideas into the sand. His jumble of crow's feet would be the beginning of the field of study which we know as psychology. This man asked himself why it is that people end up being so different, despite the fact that they all live under the same sky? How could people be different when they go to the same schools, and live in the same village? Why are we all both *alike* and *unique*?

This isn't some new species we've discovered. Introverts and extraverts aren't creatures from another planet. These are traits which are shared by all people on this planet, to varying degrees.

The introverted side of our personalities has traits such as:

- ✓ Preferring to have fewer, but deeper, friendships.
- ✓ Being uncomfortable about being in the spotlight.
- ✓ Finding it exhausting to make new acquaintances.

The extraverted side has traits such as:

- ✓ Wanting to be the life of the party.
- ✓ Being curious about strangers.
- ✓ Being able to focus on your work despite loud levels of background noise.

Think of it as two big piles of personality traits. You might identify with some of the traits in the introvert pile, and probably with some of the ones in the extravert pile as well. Perhaps your traits align so well with extraversion that you're confident to label yourself an extravert? There's often so much of both types in us that we can't decide which one of the two we belong to. People who have more or less equal parts introvert and extravert in them are called ambiverts. An ambiverted person, then, is somebody who's just as connected to the outside world as he or she is to the inside world (a personality type that someone once unflatteringly referred to as "the vanilla of personalities"). An ambivert is often able to shift back and forth between the two extremes, and go from independent thought processes, active listening, and deep reflection to behaving with a social orientation, spontaneously, and without fear of the spotlight in a group context. The ambivert personality type has received much attention of late, and which has proven to bring special benefits in areas like sales. The best way to describe an ambivert is to say that the term refers to somebody who is *free* (in the sense that he or she can gain energy from both social contexts and solitude).

It's estimated that approximately seventy percent of the global population clearly possess needs of *both* the extraverted and introverted varieties. The majority of these people consider themselves to be mostly extraverted. Only thirty percent are predominantly introverted or extraverted. Somebody who possessed each of the introverted or extraverted traits would be more or less a caricature of a person, but let's not forget that there are some pretty unusual people out there. Extreme introverts can spend days on end locked in their basements coding databases, without any human contact. A true extravert, on the other hand, is more like a lovesick puppy, that needs to be interacting with somebody each and every waking moment. Both of these extremes can be advantageous in the right contexts. Both personalities are suited for very special kinds of jobs.

Please note that when I describe somebody as an introvert or extravert in what follows, I'll be referring to people who consider those traits to be predominant in themselves. I'm not saying that this person is exclusively introverted or extraverted. In fact, he or she is very likely to possess a number of qualities from either side of this personality spectrum. Carl Jung said that if you meet somebody who is one hundred percent introverted or extraverted, chances are you're in a mental hospital.

Coming out of the Social Closet

The awakening

"But you're not an introvert, are you?"

My friend utters the words in a tone of voice that suggests I just told her that I've contracted shingles. I can see why people wouldn't think of me as an introvert, as I've spent many years concealing this side of myself. There's a hint of compassion in her voice, as though introversion were some kind of medical condition. While it's true that being an introvert is a chronic state, it's not a disease. Or, perhaps I should say it's not a disease yet. The American Psychological Association has discussed adding introversion to its list of mental afflictions. I'm not kidding!

Personally, it took me a long time to realize that I'm an introvert. I knew it as a child, but I didn't have a label for it at the time. Then, school distorted my ideas about what I ought to be like. In primary school, it dawned on me that I'd become something of an outsider in my class. This realization awakened a greater interest in socializing with others. This was my first taste of having to pretend to fit in. In time, this adjustment became so familiar to me that I forgot about certain aspects of my personality. Military service played its part in this as well. Finding alone time was quite a challenge when I was sharing a tent with twelve sweaty guys, and using a cardboard box in the woods for a latrine. Relaxation didn't come any easier after I overheard one of my tent mates whispering "kill them all" in his sleep. Professional life was the third phase of my social transformation. For many years, I thought my failure to enjoy social situations simply meant that I was strange in some way. I could almost feel my soul die at mingling events. If there's a hell for introverts, it's a big room where people just mingle forever. My superficial small talk was always full of strange, pretentious nonsense: "This Chablis is truly divine! The grape has a hint of foaming horse." Sometimes I'd pretend to use the bathroom just to steal a breather. Sometimes I'd pretend to send text messages, and try to look busy. At times, I tried to just endure it, and take part in everything to the fullest of my ability. I spoke quickly, with agitation, and my forehead was shiny with sweat. Sometimes, after a large party, I could feel spent for days. Afterwards, I'd curl up in a fetal position in the shower and rub myself all over with a sponge. There were plenty of clues, which I spent many years ignoring, until I found my way out of the extravert closet.

There were things in my living patterns that pretty much gave it away. I spent many years working from home as an illustrator. One of my favorite things to do was to be up all night working. When I looked outside at night, all of the other apartment buildings were dark. The feeling of being alone with my art, the music I'd chosen, and a strong cup of coffee gave me peace of mind. This was a deep sense of harmony. Sometimes, I'd just get in my car and drive. It could be four o'clock on a Wednesday morning. It was as though I was the only human on earth. Alone behind the wheel, I felt a sense of harmony. I charged my batteries as the lines in the road passed by in the darkness outside. Quite soon, I realized that not many of the people close to me could understand this behavior. I realized early on that most people simply can't relate to my way of living.

These solitary nocturnal activities had been a habit of mine since childhood. Activities free of any social elements left me free to be myself. I spent my childhood in the countryside, and grew up without any friends or siblings my own age. My brother is seven years younger than I am, so I was practically an only child. But introverts don't depend on the outside world for impressions. Our minds are already full of stories. That's also why I can't remember a time in my life when I was bored. If I forget my keys to the house and have to wait on the stoop, that's fine by me.

Sometimes, we need to peel ourselves away layer by layer, like onions, before we can find our way back to the people we started out as. Coming out as an introvert is a placid epiphany of clarity, rather than a revolution in the classic sense, where you man barricades or beat down doors. This revolution has nothing to do with how you're seen by others, it's about how you see yourself. Extraverts don't need to come out, because their behavior is already the ideal. However, I'm sure there are many people out there who are pretending to be extraverts. What follows are some points of view I subscribe to, which also happen to be typical of people with introverted personalities.

Hating travel

There seems to be a global conspiracy dedicated to perpetuating the notion that travel is always lots of fun. I've *never* felt the need to travel. There are extraverts who have seen every last corner of the world, but missed every corner of their own personalities along the way. For introverts, the opposite can be true. Tragically enough, some navel-gazers have never even left the county they grew up in. I'm not trying to say one way is better than the other, I'm just stating a fact. If you're an introvert, you're sensitive to change, and you tend to like structure. I've always been prone to travel jitters, even for very short journeys like day trips to Stockholm. Travel disturbs my living patterns. The day of the trip involves so many unpredictable variables.

From time to time, I've had to travel a lot for my work. This has made it a little easier, but I've never completely lost my discomfort with travelling. It's awkward and impractical. Shoes off, shoes on, buckle belts, button jackets. Unpack computers in front of pear-shaped security staff. Crowded seating areas, monitoring the screens for the departure gate. On the plane, you always end up between enormous railroad workers in tank tops, who keep pressing their skin up against you. Turbulence always seems timed to coincide with the service of the ridiculously hot coffee. At the airport, you find out that your luggage has been flown to Oslo, and you end up having to report this to somebody from India who doesn't understand your English.

Unwillingness to travel is a trait of mine. On the other hand, I usually enjoy the actual destination once I get there. It's more about the actual trip. I guess I'm just a homebody.

Verbal constipation

My threshold for opening my mouth is pretty high, which is evident in how frugal I am with my words. I don't enjoy speaking about superficial things with superficial acquaintances. I have a hard time approaching strangers. It's easy for me to get stuck in the doorway to a room full of strangers. On the other hand, I tend to get very involved if the topic under discussion is one that I'm passionate about.

When I was younger, I used to make sure to arrive early to parties, to save myself from having to introduce myself to a room full of people. Different people use up my energy to different degrees. Some people have a relaxed mode of speech that helps me last for the duration of a long conversation. I function the best with calm people who don't constantly seek eye contact, and who leave some empty space between their words.

Spring break

I've always avoided anything that feels like a popular celebration or nightlife scene. The spring break vibe, barbecues, and initiations where people have to wrestle in grease or dance in bubbles are all included in my definition of hell. Situations rife with superficial conversation, casual relationships, pierced navels, tribal tattoos, body shots, funny hats, and general revelry are simply not my element. I love meeting interesting people one at a time. I love talking about things that feel genuine. Just freaking out, letting go of boundaries, and releasing your inner caveman don't come naturally to introverts. The amount of alcohol required to make me dance would kill the average hippo. But I have no problem at all with hanging out in a nice lounge with some low-key music, some finger food, and drinks that aren't named anything involving sexual innuendo.

Punctuality

Many introverts, myself included, have a great respect for time. It's the hard currency of our lives. Since we want to manage our own time, we're often careful not to waste the time of others. I'm never late for a meeting or departure. I sometimes think I must have spent a whole week of my life sitting around in airports waiting for a departure, just to make sure I won't miss my flight! My mother is an introvert as well. She's a master of the art of coming up with excuses to be at the airport at least a day in advance, to make absolutely certain that you'll catch your plane. I envy my extraverted friend Anna, who packs her bag while the taxi driver sounds his horn at her from the street. It's worth knowing that studies have shown that extraverts and introverts experience time differently; extraverts experience time as passing somewhat faster than introverts do. When half an hour has passed, an extravert might experience it as though forty-five minutes had passed.

Statues

Introverts often come across as very stable. This is likely due to the fact that we're not particularly willing to voice our concerns. We also don't live out our emotions in our facial expressions, because we don't want to project them onto people around us. We mull over things carefully in our own minds *before* asking anybody for their help or input. For this reason, we can be regarded as very secure and strong of character. When an extraverted friend of mine told me about his depression, which had been caused by an identity crisis, he said "I think you might have a hard time understanding this."

This is quite flattering, but it's far from true. Beneath the surface, raging storms and mood swings plague introverts just the same as everybody else. Many are surprised to find out that studies have shown that we're generally *more* sensitive than extraverts. Many introverts are very uncomfortable with arguments. Introvert Lukas describes it this way: "My greatest challenge is having the courage to deal with conflicts. I can handle conflicts if they're about something that matters to me or to my kids. But they consume so much energy. I'd like to be able to manage more conflicts without getting so exhausted."

The difference between introverts and extraverts is that introverts internalize things first. We choke our emotions, far beneath the surface. If you raise your voice to me, I'll be thinking about it for days. I'd like to claim that the toughest people you know are probably also the softest people you know

Or, to put it in terms more Zen: I need to understand your reaction to fit it into my living patterns, so that I can regain my sense of harmony. The problem is that emotional outbursts are seldom particularly logical. I know you're not *really* this annoyed just because your lawn mower broke down. For an introvert, things can get really uncomfortable if somebody so much as raises their voice. We're very sensitive to tone of voice, mimicry, and other signs. Many introverts are remarkably good at picking up the things that other people communicate, but remain completely ignorant of what their own tone of voice and body language expresses.

Sun-mania!

Nice weather is a bit of a pain. Where I live, we only get a handful of hours of sunlight every year. And so, we're expected to do cartwheels out the window and rush to claim a good spot on the beach the moment the sun peeks out from behind the clouds. Just staying indoors is impossible if you have a family. This is why I'm sometimes known to sigh with relief when I see gray skies. "Cool, now I can sit down and do some writing without having to feel guilty about it."

Group assignments

I've never been very comfortable with group assignments. It seems to me that you always end up having to come up with unnecessary tasks just to make sure there's something for everybody to do. The whole thing just seems a bit childish. Participation and democracy slow progress. Discussions tend to end with the most eloquent person getting his or her way. The winner isn't the person who produces the best arguments, but rather the person who has the energy to argue the longest. This is usually an extravert. There's a difference between winning an argument and being right. In many group assignments, most of the actual work ends up being done by an introvert, who does it alone in his room while muttering something about how "talk is cheap."

All by myself

For some reason, I've always been more reluctant than most when it comes to asking for help. I can't quite explain why this is. I guess it's a combination of not wanting to trouble people and believing that nobody else can solve the problem better than I can. Studying introversion has made me realize that this isn't just me turning into a grouchy old man, and that reluctance to ask for help is actually known to be correlated with introversion.

Small talk

My best conversations are generally in-depth or abstract in nature. I've never managed to pull off that thing where you just walk up to a stranger and say "How about that game last night?". They might have actually seen the game, and then they'll find out that I don't know what the score was, or even if the sport in question is played with a ball or a puck. I prefer conversations about a different kind of topic. I usually do best when I meet somebody who shares my interests. Unfortunately, this often gets me into trouble in mingling situations. There aren't too many people who appreciate it when you start a conversation by asking them if they've considered the fact that we all die alone.

Extravert Anna says: "Sometimes, it can feel as though an introvert will only listen to you if what you're saying interests them personally. It seems a bit selfish in a way. Everything people say doesn't have to be interesting, sometimes people just need to have somebody listen to them. They need to get it out of their systems. Conversations that start out pretty dull can sometimes become interesting after a while. By the time this happens, an introvert will already have moved on, either physically or in his or her mind.

Over-analysis

All too often, I slip into my own world of concerns and worries. I carry a bubble of calm around, from which I over-analyze and over-rationalize the things that happen around me. Outside of this peaceful bubble, there's usually the ordinary relationship drama with a significant other who's annoyed at my constant daydreaming. Having difficulties seizing the moment is a strong characteristic of introverts. It has to do with how the introverted brain captures impressions from the outside world. We reflect on things that have happened, and deliberate over things that are going to happen. This bubble is useful in certain contexts, i.e., when analytical thinking is required, but it's a disadvantage in other contexts, i.e., the rest of the time.

Super focus

It's easy for me to lose myself in things, and become completely absorbed by them. It's as though my brain chooses a topic without asking me for any input, and then makes me obsess over it. I developed a total fixation with paranormal phenomena in second grade. When my classmates were on their way to each other's houses to play cowboys, I was lugging heavy books home from the library. I would sit at home and read with passionate zeal. My lively imagination turned these books into doorways to new worlds. I could spend hours on end with them.

And this hasn't changed. Whether it's working out, video games, or some type of knowledge, I can immerse myself deeply in a topic in a very short time. This behavior can verge on the manic. Introverts consume information greedily, and isolate themselves with it. My brain has an easy time registering impersonal data, but I sometimes have no idea at all what's going on in the room I'm in. On several occasions, I've looked for my glasses while wearing them.

This capacity to fixate on things is a classic characteristic of introverts. This is why introversion is so often correlated with academic achievement.

My extraverted friend Anna has this to say: "If I happen to pick a topic that interests you, you'll often know an extreme amount about it. I like that, because I want to learn more about things, either by discussing them or by listening."

Quiet rebel

Introverts are alone even when we're not *alone*. I realize this sounds like a contradiction. Extraverted people have an easy time finding each other, because they enjoy social contexts and meeting new people. Introverts find each other at the drinks table next to the dance floor – when we even bother to look for each other in the first place, that is. We're always in good company, because we enjoy hanging out with ourselves.

One problem we encounter in making friends is that we don't adapt to groups very well. Introverts don't change their clothes, music tastes, or attitudes to keep up with trends. This makes us outsiders in a way. Usually, somebody who doesn't conform is perceived as either a rebel or a nerd. It's a real fine line. We'd rather be alone and not have any friends, than have lots of friends and betray our own sense of integrity.

I think most people have the number of friends they want to have. What I mean by that is that we spend our time and energy on the things that matter to us. A large network of acquaintances will demand maintenance, which takes time. You're expected to call, email, remember birthdays, and stay in touch with the people in your network. All of this time will have to be taken from some other aspect of your life, usually from your *alone time*.

A friend of mine put it this way: "I don't like acting sociable, but I also don't like not having any friends."

In closing

Some of the traits I've discussed here are part of the definition of introversion, like preferring independent assignments. Some of the traits I've mentioned are related to introversion, without actually being features of it. Being punctual is not an introverted characteristic per se, but there is a correlation: if you encounter one of the two, your chances of finding the other are good. You could compare it with how being overweight isn't the same thing as having a heart attack, but does correlate to it, in that people who have heart attacks are often overweight.

A mother once asked me: "Is there anything I can do about my child's introversion?"

I understand where she's coming from. Parents want the best for their kids. Sometimes it feels as though being more extraverted would make my life easier. After all, for most of us, everyday life involves some degree of social interaction. The answer I gave her was "No, and yes."

I'll explain this rather cryptic response in the next chapter.

Summary for extraverts

✓ Introverts don't identify strongly with groups. This makes us independent thinkers.
✓ Introverts don't get bored as easily as extraverts.
✓ Introverts are often perceived as stable and stoic by the people around them. We experience powerful emotions beneath the surface. We're generally more sensitive and neurotic than extraverts. Hurtful comments affect us particularly severely.

Time Travel to an Unexpected Destination

There have always been ideals within the culture that influence our ideas about what makes a *real* man or woman. It used to be that introverted ideals were dominant. John Wayne's bow-legged macho characters rarely uttered more than the words "Howdy, pilgrim." Stone-faced Humphrey Bogart cynically stated that "Things are never so bad they can't be made worse." Greta Garbo didn't try to hide her introversion, and her most famous quote expresses it plainly: "I want to be alone."

The people on the silver screen have always held a strange power over our ideals. The plots of the movies of the 1950s revolved around heroic deeds, loyalty, and duty to the nation. The values of the day encouraged people to act, *not* talk, and this is why the war heroes were so often doers rather than talkers. Silence is golden. Restraint and modesty were the core virtues of the age. Great significance was attached to professional titles. People's social status determined the weight of their words in conversation. Nobody dared to question a teacher's authority in the schools of the 1950s. Children were taught never to interrupt adults, and often to refrain from speaking at all. It's easy to see how out of place talkative, outgoing, and socially oriented behavior might have seemed. It was the extraverts who were oppressed in those days. People who grew up at that time will often go to great lengths to make sure nobody tries to celebrate their birthdays. This is probably motivated by their discomfort about being in the spotlight.

In the 1950s, this whole social order was turned on its head. It all started on a bus in the South of the USA. A woman in the colored section refused to give up her seat to a white man, although she was required to do so by law at the time. Rosa Parks became a symbol of a movement of change that would leave its mark on the entire decade that followed. In the end, it came to involve so much more than segregation laws in the US: the right to freely express your opinion, the rights of all citizens to be informed about the actions of their governments, and, more than anything else, the equal value of human beings irrespective of their gender, skin tone, or sexuality. In essence, the 1960s were all about one single thing: *the individual*.

Because of this, extraverted aspects of human psychology were suddenly held up as exemplary. The ability to speak spontaneously, and express your opinion whenever the opportunity arose, became a social advantage. This populist era of politics brought about a growing interest in discussing and arguing about particular issues. This entire revolution was fueled by a wave of connectedness that brought people together in groups to manifest, protest, and take action. Also abandoned at this time was the ideal of sacrificing yourself for the good of the collective. In this new era, people's duties were more geared towards self-realization and "sticking it to the man." This is why the children of the 1960s were taught to speak their minds even if adults might disapprove.

The age of the gold star for effort

The respect enjoyed by authority figures diminished somewhat in the West. For instance, in Sweden, we implemented "Du-reformen", a linguistic reform in which titles were eliminated from everyday speech, and more informal forms of address were introduced. Old ideas about following in your parents' footsteps were gone with the wind. Children began to be taught to always seek out whatever genuinely interests them, and to feel no loyalty to anybody but themselves. This has only become more and more pronounced in the decades that have passed since the

1960s. The children of the 1990s were taught that they can become absolutely anything they want, as long as they try hard enough. This age has occasionally seen extraversion and individualism degenerate into what psychologists refer to as narcissism. This is a term used to describe an extreme focus on the self, in which somebody places him- or herself at the center of the universe. Here's a test, in case you're wondering if you might be among the afflicted:

1. Think about yourself.
2. If you got this far, you're not a narcissist.

Narcissists tend to overestimate their own ability. An American study showed that seventy percent of teenagers today feel they belong to the top ten percent of all people in terms of talent. A third of people born in the nineties also believe that they'll be celebrities during their lifetimes. Some claim that the increasingly extraverted zeitgeist of our age has produced an army of narcissists.

From Don Johnson to Don Draper

The media has helped inflate the extraverted ideal. Razor-witted extraverts like Eddie Murphy, Tom Cruise, and Michael J Fox carried Hollywood on their shoulders throughout the 1980s. Hard-boiled detectives of few words gave way to the disco cops of *Miami Vice*. Crockett and Tubbs struck poses in white loafers and expressed male vulnerability, but they were also machismo incarnate whenever an opportunity to wave their automatic pistols around presented itself. In the 1990s, we followed the outgoing characters of *Friends* as they oscillated between café tables and the apartments they shared. The music business has become a rallying point for extremely hyper-extraverted personalities. A good example of this is when Lady Gaga wore that dress made of meat. The stars of our time have taken the media stunts Madonna used to pull decades ago, and given them a massive dose of steroids. Psychologist Jean Twenge has performed longitudinal studies of extraversion, and claims that the lives of teenagers today are eighty-three percent more extraverted than they were in the 1940s. She doesn't believe that the cause of this is some change in our genetics; her theory is that many introverts today simply *believe* themselves to be extraverts, and act accordingly. Our society forces us all into an extraverted mold.

I mentioned the rise of introversion earlier. To help you understand this idea, I'd like to draw your attention to a change that has occurred in the media over the last few years. TV shows like *The Sopranos* reintroduced the old macho ideals, but with some significant differences added to the mix. The introverted Tony Soprano is unhappy, quiet, and withdrawn. He's stony exterior and broken inside all rolled up together.

During a shoot for the movie *Brokeback Mountain*, Heath Ledger asked director Ang Lee how to play his introverted character, and all Ang did was clench his fist tightly and say: "Like this."

The comedy *Napoleon Dynamite* from 2004 has become a cult classic. Napoleon is an unusual and introverted young man, whose interests include drawing Ligers – a cross between tigers and lions – and practicing his nunchuck skills. The film presents a caricature of introversion. The plot revolves around the election for student council president. *Napoleon Dynamite* is a movie about nerds, and kids simply love it. A millennial I discussed this with recently said that "nerdy is the new black". It's considered cool to be quiet and submerge yourself in special interests.

The TV show *The Big Bang Theory* boldly proclaims its alliance with the introverted side of things, a move that has made it incredibly popular. As they say on the show: "Come to the Nerd-Side, we have Pi." Perhaps what makes these shows so successful is the fact that many of the newly awakened introverts identify with this nerdy ideal. Introverts in the media are no longer portrayed as obsessive trekkies or crazy cat ladies. AMC's *Mad Men* is one of the most successful TV shows of all time. It tells the story of Don Draper, a secretive and introverted charmer who looks painfully good in a suit. He chain smokes, broods, cheats with impunity, and drinks his way through each episode. Don Draper doesn't speak much, is hard to pin down, and is brilliant at his work.

Holy flypaper Batman!

It's interesting to follow characters through decades of media appearances. Batman is a good example of this, and the transformations he's gone through speak volumes about how society's view of introversion has changed. In the forties, Batman was a hardened lone avenger, who shot and killed bad guys like it was nobody's business. He was a character void of all empathy. Then, in the 1960s, the dominant mood of the day forced Batman to come out of his shell. Movies and TV shows from this era present a comfortably out-of-shape dude in a costume, who feeds frighteningly square nuggets of wisdom to his young ward Robin.

> Robin: "You can't get away from Batman that easy!"
> Batman: "Easily."
> Robin: "Easily."
> Batman: "Good grammar is essential, Robin."
> Robin: "Thank you."
> Batman: "You're welcome."

This Batman is a sociable goody two-shoes. He and Robin are suspiciously friendly with one another, and when this was pointed out by a concerned psychologist at the time, the character Batgirl was invented before you could say "Holy

Damage Control!" The Batman of the 1960s is a casual, playful extravert who doesn't mind showing off a little. He dances, sings, and even surfs in the TV show.

Now, the circle is complete, and the original Batman has returned. The recently completed film trilogy features a Batman whose soul is as black as night. The reticent recluse is back, and there's not a trace of Robin to be found. Today's Batman is an introverted weirdo, who utters something like four lines in total over the course of the movie.

Introverts in the movies

Some movies have that special something that grabs my interest from the very first moment. Sometimes, it's a special blend of imagery and characters that draws me in. The movies I like all share a common denominator: they seem to appeal to my introverted aspects.

I was in my teens when *Edward Scissorhands* hit the theaters. It arrived in an era of movie history when most of the films being produced were about muscles, fire, and vengeance. The characters in the vengeance movies were as thin as prison toilet paper, and the dialog was mostly one liners, like the classic "Yippie ki-ai motherf***er" of *Die Hard. Edward Scissorhands* defied this trend.

Edward's story is a phenomenal modern take on the story of Pinocchio. Edward is an extremely sensitive young man, who's left alone in a big old mansion when his creator dies before having time to finish his hands. For some reason, while he was waiting for his real hands, the decision was made to replace them with scissors for the time being. A kind-hearted family finds Edward, and adopts him as their own. The introverted Edward's fumbled attempts at social interaction are touching. This is a beautiful and sad story, which is well worthy of reflection.

Last decade, the masterpiece *Lost in Translation* hit the screens. This movie portrays a brief relationship between two introverted people, who both feel that there's something missing from their lives. The main characters are very convincingly played by Scarlett Johansson and Bill Murray. Most of the movie's action takes place in a hotel in Japan, and the dialog is sparse. The atmospheric Japanese ambiance and the relaxed tempo lull the viewer into a mild trance for one hundred minutes. This was the first time I ever saw a movie portray a relationship in such a down-to-earth and understated way. *Lost in Translation* was an experience that would stick in my mind for a long time.

Granted, a number of introverted characters had appeared in movies before this. Yoda, of the Star Wars series, is a green goblin who's two feet tall and nine hundred years old, and lives all alone in a swamp. That doesn't exactly scream "extravert", does it?

The character Travis Bickle in *Taxi Driver* (1976) is an introverted man who struggles with insomnia and the pressures of not fitting in with society. In the movie, he descends into a spiral of paranoid delusions, which eventually erupt in the story's macabre climax.

Jean-Pierre Jeunet's *Amélie* is a work of cinematic genius. It follows the innocent Amélie, a quiet dreamer who sees the world through the eyes of a child. In a memorable scene, we see her go to enormous effort to prepare for a date with a guy. But when he shows up, she's unable to say a single word to him. I think many introverts can relate to this.

Stieg Larsson broke new ground for introverts in Swedish literature. The character Lisbeth Salander from his books is an iconic recluse. She doesn't have many lines in the movies, and speaks mainly through her actions.

Clint Eastwood bids us adieu in *Gran Torino* (2011). The introverted character he plays here is conceptualized as an aged version of the macho characters he used to play decades ago. Gran Torino is a sentimental goodbye from an introverted male ideal that is all but extinct.

41

Movies impact our values more than we realize. The great number of introverted characters in the last few decades has begun to affect our ideas concerning what's *normal.*

Fight your apathy, or don't

When I grew up, there was still plenty of room for people to be introverts. In the 1980s, the predominant parenting style afforded children a great degree of freedom. Then, our teen years arrived, and it was time for us to form our identities. We looked around for role models to show us what to be like. Unfortunately, the stars of our age were mostly just addicts with instruments. Guns N'Roses, Mötley Crüe, and all those grunge bands gave us a pretty bleak outlook on things. If I had to use a single word to describe the requisite for being popular when I was a teenager, it would be "apathy". Our youth culture was based on the idea that *not* caring was cool. While this attitude may not be the best, apathy can also be a source of calm. It's easy to lean back and relax when you have no ambitions or hopes for the future. I had my share of negative experiences during the last few summers of my youth, but there wasn't much stress. In many ways, school was easy for somebody with an introverted personality. You could sleep through the classes, and then cram for the exams. If you aced the test, you'd get the top grade. The grading system was simple, logical, and about as sophisticated as a plate of hash browns. For somebody like me, who had decent memory skills, it was easy to do well at the subjects that caught my interest. Unfortunately, there weren't many of those. We basically never had to do group assignments at school. We all sat at our desks, facing the front of the room. It was extremely rare for us to be expected to speak before the whole class, which was probably a good thing, since the presentations were always about somebody's hamster anyway. The teaching profession was in its last decade of enjoying some semblance of authority.

Planet Ego

Twenty years later, the situation has changed completely. Youth culture has made a radical move in a completely different direction. Our idols are all beautiful people, who represent wholesome ideals and encourage us to have the courage to follow our dreams. Each and every Katy Perry out there is helping kids believe in themselves and develop their talents. These performers don't OD on heroin every other day, or act psychotic, like celebrities did in the 1980s. Performers these days tend to promote positive values. They teach their fans to believe in themselves, to be tolerant of each other's differences, and to stand up for their opinions. In the media, talent shows like *American Idol* and *So You Think You Can Dance* attract top ratings. Young people compete and show off their talents for performing arts of all kinds, from opera singing to playing the nose flute. Youth culture has never been so intensely oriented towards promoting ambition and physical appearance before. It's more important than ever to look good, to find your own style, and to have ambitious goals for your future. An army of beauty queens smiles anxiously as they march towards a future so brightly lit up by their own expectations that they have to wear shades to face it. This cutthroat competition for attention is the reason why extraversion is flourishing so. If you're not being heard, you're not being seen. It used to be that people who were special became famous, but now people want to make themselves special by becoming famous.

The change that the schools have gone through has only contributed to making this such an extraverted age. Group assignments make up a growing proportion of schoolwork. Today, simply *writing* good work won't cut it. No, the important thing is that you're able to step up and *speak* to your class about it. You also need to be able to present rhetorical arguments in support of your conclusions.

Subjects like rhetoric and presentation technique are included in the curriculum today. The solid grading system of the past is gone, and an element of negotiation has been allowed into the practice of grading. Persistent parents often phone teachers to demand that their kids' grades be raised. A lot of people seem to believe that you can achieve anything as long as you raise your voice enough, and most of the time, they're right. Social relationships between teachers and students are more important than ever. These days, the students who get the best grades are usually the outgoing entrepreneurial types, who have the gift of the gab and good networking skills.

Revenge of the nerds

There are other signs that the old values are returning, apart from the various ways in which the media has flirted with introversion. In some respects, we're becoming more quiet, and less adventurous. People are getting married earlier now than they did a decade ago. A growing number of young people consider a life as a homemaker a viable option. Family ties are becoming the central concern, rather than careers. Moving to the countryside, to be closer to nature, is a growing trend. A Swedish survey from 2011 showed that seven out of ten women between the ages of fifteen and twenty-nine would consider moving to the countryside.

There's also another factor that has contributed to the rise of introversion. In the past, introverts used to sit in their rooms creating amazing stuff. The problem was that they didn't have the skills required to sell their creations to rowdy crowds. Strong ideas were easily overlooked when the voices promoting them were weak. These days, the Internet allows introverts' products to reach the general public without their inventors ever having to make eye contact with people or make awkward cold calls. A piece of writing or a picture can be distributed to millions of people with just a press of a button. If something is good, it takes on a life of its own in the social media, and goes viral. An example of this is when Markus Persson sat at home coding a game all by himself. The game would eventually be given the title *Minecraft*, and ended up making him 2.5 billion dollars when he sold it to Microsoft in 2014. Introverts' talents are more viable these days than they were back when everything seemed to be rigged in favor of the extraverts. It's worth pointing out that recently, a number of seemingly introverted natures have taken leading roles in global politics. Barack Obama, for instance, has a low-key, laconic, and focused personality, which is a hallmark of introversion.

Our culture is becoming more tolerant of introversion. John Wayne is on his way back, and perhaps we're finally about to see a job listing specifically ask for an introverted person; somebody who can keep everything in his or her mind at once, and enjoys being positioned at the periphery of the network.

Summary for extraverts

- ✓ In previous decades, social norms favored introversion. In the last fifty years, extraverted behavior has been promoted as the ideal.
- ✓ A number of signs indicate that we're past the peak of this extraverted era, and that the age we're about to enter will be a more introverted one.
- ✓ The Internet is the ideal sales channel for introverts, because it allows them to show their ideas to the world without having to raise their voices.

The Introvert and Extravert Psyches

I remember flying up the pine wood stairs. The heavy load I carried felt like a sack of goose feathers. After spending twenty-four hours hanging out with my cousins, I'd been royally rewarded by my comic collecting uncle: he'd filled a shopping bag with graphic fiction goodness, and given it to me. I had only recently learned to read; a skill I had acquired very quickly. I felt a constant craving for things to read. I got into bed immediately, and turned my reading light on. The stories cast their spells on me, and I lost track of time. The Phantom, Spider-Man, Donald Duck, Archie - to me, these were real people of flesh and blood. Suddenly, it was dark outside, and I had no idea how time had gone by so quickly. When I finally went to sleep, my head was spinning with characters, stories, and reflections. Most of all, I remember feeling completely relaxed. Although I didn't know the meaning of the word at the time, I was in a state of total Zen.

Introversion is biologically determined. It has to do with the level of activity that's required before your hormones tell your brain that you've had enough. Extraverts require higher levels of activity. Something that's fun and stimulating for an introvert can seem dull and uneventful to an extravert. This is why the cliché about introverts living at home until they're forty-five and spending all their money on model railways is true to some extent. People like that do exist. The idea that extraverts are adrenaline junkies who need to ride shopping carts down cliff sides in South America just to feel alive is true of some people, too. Which level of activity you enjoy depends on your need for social interaction. Conversing with a group might seem like a peaceful thing to do. But in any social situation, the brain is bombarded with huge amounts of information. It's been said that communicating with others requires us to maintain 247 simultaneous thought processes at once. We take in such an enormous load of stuff during conversations: we observe hand gestures, mimicry, tone of voice, posture, pupils and so on; we listen, evaluate, and relate to what we're being told; and we ponder the things that aren't being said, and try to read between the lines. An introverted psyche will soon be overloaded by all this. One study arrived at the conclusion that introverts get exhausted because we take in more information than extraverts do. When we get overloaded, our first reaction is to try to withdraw.

MRI scans have shown that more blood passes through the frontal regions of introverts' brains. These are the parts of the brain that handle problem solving and reflection. Extraverts, on the other hand, tend to have a greater blood flow in the areas of the brain that handle emotions and visual, olfactory, tactile, and auditory impressions. Basically, extraverts are more present in the moment. Many introverts, myself included, will probably identify with feeling like they're stuck inside a bubble sometimes. It's as though that inner voice takes charge. This manifests in our daydreaming, or losing ourselves in thought.

Extraverts are programmed to flourish from interacting with others. Being in crowds makes them euphoric and hyperactive. They like being close to the center of events. This is why extraverts lug their acoustic guitars to parties to play "Living next door to Alice".

Many extraverts speak quickly. Sometimes, they seem to be unable to filter their thoughts before they speak, which can cause them to make casual observations that they end up regretting.

> *Extravert*: "Congratulations! When are you due?"
> *Annoyed*: "Huh? No, we're not having a baby!"
> *Extravert*: "But...?" Points at stomach.
> *Really Annoyed*: "No, I'm just fat ..."
> *Extravert*: "Hey, so ... how about that game, eh?"

Extraverts will often have a very open attitude, and share things freely with you, whether you're interested or not.

Once, during a job interview, a woman told me: "My ovaries are aching something terrible today." This was the first thing she said to me after "Hello". This open attitude makes extraverts easy to get to know. They're generous with their time and attention, and trusting of strangers. With them, *what you see is what you get*, at least to some degree.

Many extraverts seem to have trouble dealing with silence during a conversation. Pauses offend their sensibilities. They've made it their mission to fill any such silences with words. You could almost call them socially incontinent. In other words, talking about the weather and other forms of shooting the breeze are all fairly extraverted acts.

Relating to activities

Imagine that your boss sticks his head into your cubicle and says:

> "Hey, I'm in a real jam! I have to be in Tokyo tomorrow for a five-day conference, but I feel like I'm coming down with something. Could you go instead of me?"

What's your immediate reaction? Does this make you feel excited, or stressed out? Introverts don't need as much variety and adventure. For us, excitement could mean finding out about the new features in the next version of Microsoft's operating system. A former colleague of mine once got so excited over successfully parallel processing his graphics cards that he had to change his pants. Extraverts, on the other hand, tend to love every kind of activity. They're always *up for it*, a bit like a Jack Russell terrier. Introverts tend rather to seek peace, or the absence of activities. Our mentalities make us more similar to fat Persian cats.

Introverts are at their happiest when they get to go to bed with an empty schedule for the next day. We love the feeling of finishing something. Extraverts hate that feeling. This introverted calm has some positive side effects. For example, my wife often struggles with getting our kids to sleep. The children throw pillows, bounce around all over the place, and frantically chew on the furniture instead of resting. It's as if her mere presence in the room was feeding them energy. If she leaves the room for a moment, something interesting happens. Within a few minutes, they'll have crept up next to me in the couch, and they soon fall asleep without any fuss. I think this is probably an effect of my calm demeanor, but she claims I put them to sleep by being "so damn boring."

This thing about the *need for activity* requires some explanation. Extraverts can have tremendous energy when it comes to social situations. The go to meetings, networking events, line dancing classes, baby yoga, and lots of other group activities, without getting tired.

Introverts have lots of energy too, but we spend it on other things than social activities. The author Stephen King is an unusually introverted person. Despite this, he's found the energy to produce more than sixty enormous novels and hundreds of short stories during his career. Introverts are energetic, but not always in the conventional sense, and this can make us seem rather secretive about our work.

To illustrate this, I'd like to point out that much of what people take to be the lazy wastefulness of computer-crazed teens actually involves great mental challenges. A woman I spoke to realized this when she began to learn more about her son's interests. At first, she thought he was just another useless teenager who was wasting his life away playing pointless games on his computer. He spent more time talking into his headset than to real people. Eventually, she came to understand that he'd been playing *World of Warcraft*, and that he regularly coordinated gaming sessions which involved several hundreds of players. There he was, casually conversing in English, which isn't his first language, with people from all around the world. While he was doing that, he was also deftly moving his fingers around the keyboard like a pianist, making strategic decisions in real time, and giving orders to people who were much older than him. Perhaps one day he'll be an air-traffic controller, and command pilots through a headset, in much the same way.

Internal vision

Do you know somebody who's a good sketch artist, writer, painter, or musician? Consider this person's social preference. Where would you place this person on the scale from introvert to extravert? The odds are pretty good that this person is an introvert.

Visual artistic talent is strongly correlated with introversion. Psychology experiments have shown that introverts are good at visualizing what they're told. We turn words into pictures. This ability to visualize is a result of our keeping one eye turned inwards. This is the positive aspect of our absent-mindedness and disconnection from the present. Artistic expression is strongly related to introversion. Art is an expression of inner life, as taken down in shorthand by the imagination. I don't just mean art in the sense of paintings and sculptures; this applies equally to music, film, poetry, and fiction writing. Over the years, I've become convinced that the greatest movie directors are all introverts. Just look at this list of names: Ingmar Bergman, Woody Allen, Liv Ullman, Stanley Kubrick, Ridley Scott, Steven Spielberg – all of these represent the quiet team.

The actor's dugout is full of introverts as well. Here, we find people like Clint Eastwood, Tom Hanks, Meg Ryan, Glenn Close, Gwyneth Paltrow, Marilyn Monroe, and Peter Sellers. How can it be that people who are averse to social situations end up choosing an occupation in which any success immediately attracts massive attention?

Why are so many actors introverts?

In social situations, introverts can sometimes get the feeling that they don't belong. This is most obvious in larger groups of people. It's as though the introverts were sitting on the bench, watching the extraverts socialize on the playing field. I guess all of those people who became directors, artists, actors, and writers accepted this. They simply picked up pen and paper, and tried to capture the things they were seeing. Woody Allen and Ingmar Bergman have both been praised for their depictions of human relations. I once spoke to an elderly gentleman who had worked in theater all his life. He told me that most of the actors he'd worked with over the years had been introverts. These people were shy of the stage, and had needed some time to grow into their roles in the spotlight.

Robert De Niro put on sixty-five pounds to play the aging boxer Jake La Motta in *Raging Bull*. Christian Bale lost much more weight than that for his role in *The Machinist*, where he plays an anorexic shard of a human being. Both of these actors are extremely meticulous about their work, and are known to stay in character completely, even between shoots or performances. They're both fantastic actors, who consider themselves to be introverts. It would be unforgivable of me to omit Meryl Streep, who's considered by many to be the most talented actress of our times. She, more than anyone else, has a reputation for fully immersing herself in the characters she plays. She's also an introvert. But the question remains: what makes an introvert choose to do this?

Here's the answer: many introverts report feeling as though they were always wearing a mask. They've internalized a learned behavior to make it easier for them to spend time with other people. And so, strangely enough, playing a role can be familiar territory to an introvert. This is why the acting profession, and many service professions, suit people like us so well. A psychologist once claimed that introverted people have two personalities: *the public one* and *the private one*. There's a lot of truth to that.

Result or relation?

It was pandemonium. There were colorful LEGO bricks and scribbled sheets of paper everywhere. None of my childhood activities depended on the participation of other people. I somehow never felt the need for that. The most important things for me were always my ideas, my imagination, and my thoughts. I was after the results, not the relationship. I once built an awesome LEGO space base with my cousin. It was an enormous structure, which covered most of the floor of my room. The moment we were finished, I wanted to tear it down and build something new. But to my extraverted cousin, the whole point of building it had been to play with it. I remember this moment, because it's such a good illustration of what has remained my general outlook to this day: creating things is more interesting than spending time with other people. In the eyes of an extravert, this makes me somewhat antisocial, and a bit of a lone wolf.

Extraversion and introversion can be observed in our behavior at just a few months of age. If you drip lemon juice onto the tongue of an extraverted baby, it'll keep its mouth open, to get more of the sour sensation. Introverts, on the other hand, tend to get overstimulated and close their mouths. Research studies have investigated how babies of four months react to popping balloons. These studies, which have since become legendary, were performed by a scientist called Jerome Kagan. Research was a lot easier to do before the 1950s, because the concepts of ethics and morals hadn't been invented yet, and nobody thought twice about performing all kinds of experiments on babies. Kagan found that some of the children were frightened by the balloons, while others didn't react much. A few decades later, he contacted the same children again. He found that the ones

53

who'd had the strongest reactions were introverts, and the ones who hadn't been frightened were extraverts. Longitudinal studies of this kind have given us a very clear idea of how extremely well-defined this personality trait is. From about the age of two, symptoms begin to appear. I can see these differences quite plainly in my own children. My son Ludde likes to play on his own, but he's startled by noises, while my daughter Smilla needs constant affirmation and isn't frightened of anything (except for woodpeckers, which are the object of an irrational phobia of hers).

I don't need to look any further than to myself to realize how long-lasting these traits are. My children have Duplo LEGO, with the larger bricks that are suitable for small children. My daughter often brings this LEGO out to play, and then I have no choice but to indulge her. I'll often come to my senses an hour later, after I've finished building a perfect replica of the Space Needle. By then, my daughter has gotten bored and moved on to the next room to watch TV. To put it in simple terms, I still have that longing to create things and immerse myself in stuff. Immersion is a central concept in the life of an introvert. That's is why I'm still so dependent on reading. Reading is a way for me to ease my mind.

Extraverts need activity

There's a girl I know who's traveled more than anybody else I've met. She's fed killer whales, hugged grizzly bears, had diarrhea in the Amazon jungle, and traveled across Alaska in a dog sled. She's a very extraverted person, who's always on the move, and always in the mood to hang out. There's nothing she loves more than the unexpected, and she always leaves room in her calendar for spontaneous adventures. Last summer, she was asked to take care of a bus load of soccer hooligans. She replied "Sure!", and a few hours later, found herself working as a tour guide for the first time in her life. She spent the next day and night in the company of about thirty soccer fans. She was rubbing shoulders with new people almost every day during that time. Just the thought of having to endure that hurts my introverted soul. When she got home, she unpacked, and did some laundry. She took a few breaths, and aired her apartment out a little. The next day, she booked a last-minute vacation.

She's a good example of a strongly extraverted person. She's curious about life, and hungry for more of the world. Extraverts are addicted to life; they're always on the lookout for their next social fix.

My brother is another example of an extravert. There's always some project on the go in his life, always some activity in his pipeline. When he's alone, he calls someone. His network is enormous. Growing up, all I ever heard was: "Hey, aren't you Anton's big brother?

Extraverts shine around other people. Mingling excites them; their energy goes through the roof, their mood peaks, and they hope the night will never end. Extraverts appreciate spontaneity.

"Let's do something crazy? Just go somewhere!"
"What for?" asks the introvert, who enjoys planning and preparation, and enjoys peace and quiet even more.
"Come on, let's do this!" He's acting a little manic.
"What did you say this was called'?" My eyebrows are somewhere close to my hairline.
"Tequila Suicide!" He smiles from ear to ear.
"Eh?"
"Here's what you do: put the lemon in your eye, snort the salt, and drink the tequila!"
"Why are we doing this again?" I ask.
"Stop being so damned boring! Try to live a little!"

My friend's definition of "living a little" includes drinking until your vocabulary is reduced to a handful of vowels.

Extraverts are drawn to activity; introverts are drawn to stillness. For this reason, introverts are rarely bored. This could be the single most important difference between introverts and extraverts.

An introverted giant

Finally, Hans Eysenck emerged from the airport terminal. He'd just spent ten hours on a transatlantic flight. His body was weary with age and cancer, but his gaze was as keen as ever. His old friend professor Thayer was waiting for him. Thayer asked him what he did during the flight. Hans answered quietly: I thought.

Hans Eysenck is quoted in more books and articles than Freud and Jung. His contributions to the field constitute a magnificent body of research. Eysenck was the first person to successfully connect biology with psychology. You could say that he put the finishing touches to a joint effort that had been in the works for more than 2,500 years. The earliest ideas about personalities we know of were written down in pre-Christian times by Hippocrates, who was the first to chart the different personality types.

Then, a couple of millennia down the road, Freud and Jung took up where he left off. Hans Eysenck was the first to apply the scientific method to this theory.

He basically took Jung's and Freud's definitions of extraversion and introversion, and examined them with the aid of modern tools. Freud and Jung were philosophers rather than psychologists, and they most definitely weren't scientists. This means that they occasionally expressed their ideas in incredibly abstract ways.

Jung defined introversion and extraversion based on whether an individual replenishes her energy by spending time alone or by spending time with others. Freud considered introversion a trait that was mainly a matter of self-control. Eysenck decided to determine two things:

- ✓ Whether this trait really existed, or was simply a philosophical myth
- ✓ What the physiological manifestation of this preference was

Hans Eysenck performed an extended and multi-faceted series of studies of introversion over several decades. Among other things, he subjected introverts and extraverts to isolation, and measured and compared the time it took for them to become too stressed to continue the experiment.

He discovered that the traits identified by his predecessors could be traced back to various hormonal levels. They used MRI technology to observe the differences in blood flow in the brains of introverts and extraverts. The need for sleep, reactions to stress, thought processes, and perceptual abilities all proved to be connected to this preference. In one of the studies, the working capacities of introverts and extraverts who'd been denied sleep for thirty-six hours were measured and compared. It turned out that the extraverts' performance was far worse than it had been in a fully rested state, but that the introverts managed to maintain almost the same capacity as before. One of the theories put forth to explain this is that the introverted brain is resource-efficient, i.e., that it expends less energy than the extraverted brain. In this respect, introverts are more like marathon runners than sprinters.

Hans Eysenck is described as a stubborn introvert who likes to question received truths. He would debate for hours on end, without backing down so much as an inch. His opinions were backed up by firm convictions. One of the more infected debates was sparked when he claimed that psychotherapy serves no useful purpose.

When Eysenck wasn't caught up in some scientific battle or other, he was an intensely productive man, who wrote eighty books and hundreds of reports during his lifetime.

People have described him as a quiet and modest person, who often left his own name out of research papers to promote the efforts of others. Colleagues have told of how he insisted on putting their names down as the sole authors of reports they had written together. Hans Eysenck passed on in 1997.

There's a collection of anecdotes on his website, in which past colleagues and students describe the man's personality. The combined picture they present is that of an introverted, generous, and insanely brilliant man.

Stability

Eysenck introduced a new dimension to the concepts of introversion and extraversion by discovering another aspect that was also deserving of study. He called it *stability*. A person who has high stability is different from a person with low stability in a number of ways. Psychologists call the dimension of stability *neuroticism*; a term used to describe a person's tendency to experience and display negative emotions. A neurotic person is more likely to feel angry, depressed, or pessimistic.

Eysenck believed that this dimension was what determined whether introversion or extraversion would end up being beneficial to an individual or not. Take being sociable, for example. It could be considered to be the strongest trait in extraverts. If you're sociable and stable, you like people, and enjoy the dialogs you have with them. You're observant of others, and interested in what they have to say. If you're sociable but not stable, that means you tend rather to feed off of people in the same way that vampires feed on blood. You want an audience that listens to you and acknowledges your needs, but you're not very interested in what other people are thinking. Eysenck borrowed the names for his four personality types from Hippocrates' theory from 2,500 years ago. They are: choleric, phlegmatic, sanguine, and melancholy.

A stable person reaps all of the benefits of his or her orientation, while an unstable one will display its drawbacks.

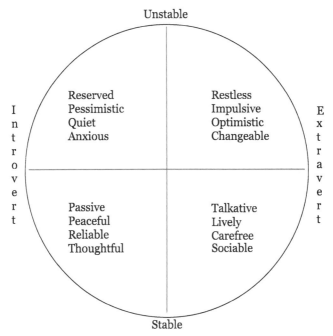

Defining characteristics of Eysenck's four personality types.

Extraverted and unstable – choleric
Examples: Lucy, Miss Piggy, Donald Duck, John McEnroe.

Lucy from the *Peanuts* cartoons is a pretty iconic portrayal of the choleric personality. This is somebody who is outgoing and temperamental. She lets people know her feelings, reacts to things immediately, and bases her opinions on her gut reactions. Cholerics will often dominate the people around them in a negative way. They're somewhat fickle, and prone to quick changes of heart. Cholerics are difficult people to deal with, because their tempers, opinions, and values keep changing all the time. They attach great weight to status and prestige, and find titles very important.

Introverted and stable – phlegmatic
Examples: Linus, Buddha, Gandhi, Winnie the Pooh, Morgan Freeman, Hillary Clinton.

These are calm and secure people with firmly rooted self-images. They have little need for self-assertion, or drawing attention to themselves. This kind of introvert is often thought to be a good listener, a thoughtful decision maker, or a wise old lady. Phlegmatics have reflective and analytic minds, with very unbiased and uncompromising thought processes. As leaders, they show a lot of faith in their co-workers. Phlegmatics give the people around them a chance to try their wings and shine.

Extraverted and stable – sanguine
Examples: Snoopy, Jesus, Tigger, Will Smith, Oprah Winfrey.

This is the extraverted personality at its absolute best – characterized by its positive and optimistic outlook on life. Sanguines have faith in the people around them. They like other people for the right reasons. They don't think of them as tools for achieving influence or status. A sanguine is considerate, includes others in conversations, and keeps the mood friendly. Being helpful without expecting anything in return is a sanguine trait.

Introverted and unstable – melancholy
Examples: Charlie Brown, Ior, Woody Allen, Marilyn Monroe.

When the introverted aspect is matched with poor self-esteem, an anxious personality shines through. This is a person who thinks of change as a threat, and strangers as competitors. She experiences her life through a pessimistic filter, and she tends to avoid any contact with people she doesn't know. Cynicism is a common feature among the melancholy, and they see hidden motives in the behavior of others, even when it seems to be beyond reproach in every way.

HSP – the Highly Sensitive Person

In recent years, many pages have been written about the mysterious concept of a *Highly Sensitive Person*. This is usually abbreviated HSP, and describes a personality type that's said to make up fifteen percent of the population. HSP was discovered by Elaine Aron in 1996. Her research can be regarded as a continuation of Hans Eysenck's attempts to reduce behavior to biology. HSP shares some of the most typical characteristics of introversion, which is why I'm including it here. Of the highly sensitive, about seventy percent are introverts. I'd like to emphasize that there are several personality traits that differ between HSP and introversion.

Basically, HSP is about having very sensitive perception, a nervous system that's easily overloaded. HSP is an innate disposition involving a great focus on sensory data such as smells, tastes, sounds, or images. This heightened sensitivity means that a HSP is easily overstimulated. They perceive smells as too powerful, or noises as too loud, long before non-HSPs experience any discomfort. One HSP I know will wash her entire fridge out if a bowl of olives smells just the slightest bit suspicious. HSPs have more sensitive reward systems than extraverts, which makes them prone to strong emotional reactions. Highly sensitive people are easily fascinated by little details. They share this characteristic with introverts, who are good with details, and have a high tolerance for monotony, as I've mentioned previously. A highly sensitive person gets exhausted from interacting with people, just like an introvert. A core characteristic of highly sensitive individuals is their big bleeding hearts. They empathize strongly with others. However, this gift can also be a burden, as a HSP will often internalize the bad moods of others, and be affected by them. Some people claim that HSPs are overrepresented among people who suffer burnout as a result of stress.

A simplified description of HSP would be that it's a condition in which certain personality traits are turned up to eleven. Typical HSP characteristics are openness to impressions, meticulousness, imagination, low stress tolerance, and strong empathy.

Common to introversion and HSP:

- ✓ Sensitivity to stimuli, and low thresholds for stress and distraction
- ✓ Don't get bored easily, and find pleasure in small things
- ✓ Find interactions with people tiring
- ✓ Focus on details and quality
- ✓ Think for a long time, and don't like making hasty decisions

Exclusive to HSP:

- ✓ Suffer sensory overload easily, and are sensitive to subtle things that others won't even notice, such as scents or disturbing background noises
- ✓ A great sense of presence which makes them very attentive to what's going on in the moment (an extraverted characteristic)

- ✓ Lively inner emotions, and a tendency to be consumed by strong emotions of both the positive and negative varieties
- ✓ An empathic radar that picks up on the moods of others, and an ability to sense the things that are left unsaid

It's hard not to wonder *why* nature makes us introverts, extraverts, ambiverts, HSPs, and so on. Why aren't we all just extraverts instead?

One biologist has suggested that the explanation could be that evolution likes to hedge its bets. Each personality type has its own particular strengths. If we mix them, we'll end up with one group of people who are curious, reactive, and spontaneous – extraverts. Another group will be reflective, cautious and wary – introverts. HSPs will provide the group with their own distinct set of virtues. Nature likes variety, basically.

Pigeonholing people

A long time ago, in a country far, far away, I decided to treat going to work like going to a costume party. I had told myself that it would be easy for me to get away with wearing a loud costume. This was before my interest in psychology awakened, before I knew the first thing about personality traits. I had a coworker who seemed painfully slow and convoluted to me, both in his thoughts and his speech. No matter what I asked him, he would think for ages before responding. It seemed to me that he disliked all kinds of change. He seemed to think that it was his job to make sure everything remained in the exact same state that it was already in. This could be quite frustrating to a young buck who saw the potential for improvement in everything around him. Whenever we spoke to each other, I felt the urge to complete his sentences, because he spoke so slowly.

This ended up making him like me just as much as I liked him – that is, not at all. Then, I was sent to my first personal development class. There, I took a personality test, which provided me with my first opportunity to reflect on how I behaved in comparison to others. I was surprised to discover that I had *a personality*. I'd known who I was all my life, of course, but I'd never thought of myself as more deliberate, dependent on routine, or results-oriented than the average person. I'd never thought of myself as somebody who had a lesser need for social interaction than the people around me. This was the strange thing: Before I took my first personality test, I thought I was average in every sense, a true everyman. Then, I learned about introversion and extraversion. This changed how I perceived others in a way that seemed magical: my slow, meticulous, and sluggish co-worker was suddenly just an introvert to me, thanks to my new understanding of the world. The very moment I categorized him this way, he became an asset instead. I began to use his thoughtfulness to evaluate my own thinking. His strengths turned into a way of improving my own results. I'd ask him: "What do you think about this?", and then give him all the time in the world to think it over.

No matter how open-minded and modern we like to think we are, we should realize that we generalize all the time. Our brains have absolutely phenomenal built-in features for this. It might sound a little odd, but a lot of research has indicated that generalization is one of the most sophisticated of the functions of the human brain. Generalizations are heuristic shortcuts, which allow us to make quick assumptions without having to assimilate large quantities of information. Many people are relieved to be given a label to apply to themselves. A childhood friend of mine was diagnosed with ADHD as an adult, and found great relief in this. Suddenly, he was able to see that the traits which he'd struggled with his entire life weren't just immature nonsense, but aspects of a neurological condition.

Even people who consider themselves open-minded, and

strongly oppose generalization, are guilty of generalizing all the time. On several occasions, I've been locked in discussion with somebody categorically opposed to all kinds of generalization. A wise woman once said: "Before we can confront our prejudices, we have to acknowledge them first."

I think generalizations need to be loose and casual. They should be easy to amend, and most importantly tolerant, because every individual you encounter is a potential exception to the rule. For instance, you're not an introvert to the exclusion of all else. You're lots of things. Maybe you're somebody's big brother, or little sister. Maybe you're somebody's dad or mom, and maybe that gives you certain characteristics. You could be an immigrant or an emigrant, or gay or straight. All of these are different threads in the tapestry of your personality. The exceptions make the rule. For instance, my wife Hanna is very sensitive to noises when she's concentrating. That's not typical of extraverts. In similar fashion, I don't act like a typical introvert when I'm talking about something that interests me. In those situations, people tend to perceive me as passionate, a quick speaker, and outgoing.

To me, the idea that personality traits don't exist is ridiculous. It seems completely unreasonable to believe that everybody's personality is identical at birth; that each of us is molded exactly the same. There's a kind of beauty to being able to identify myself as an introvert, instead of spending my time trying to figure out what's wrong with me.

Lukas is an introverted blogger, journalist, and father of three. He describes it like this:

> *I've felt out of place my entire life, mostly because of my introversion. I used to think that I had to like parties, that I had to like being around people all the time, and that I had to be good at small talk. My repeated failures at these things ended up harming my self-esteem and confidence.*

Strangely enough, I've become much better at being extraverted since I realized that I'm an introvert. For one thing, I can plan my extraverted adventures to ensure I won't get too fatigued by them, and for another thing, I feel secure about who I am, and proud of it, which has helped improve my confidence and self-esteem.

The concept of introversion has become enormously significant to me, perhaps because of the many years I spent living a very extraverted life, despite being a very introverted person at heart.

Not categorizing people simply means lumping them all together in a single universal category. The assumption then is usually that everybody is the same as *me*, or worse, that everybody conforms to the *societal norm*. This means that introverts can seem shy, dull, or arrogant in the eyes of an extravert. Once you've learned more about the topic, your observations will be more positive. I don't think we should be afraid of identifying patterns, as long as we remain open-minded enough to reevaluate them. Understanding increases tolerance between people who are different. As Abraham Lincoln said: I don't like that man. I must get to know him better.

Nature, or nurture, or what?

Philosopher René Descartes said: "I think, therefore I am." Existing and being able to think are perhaps the most mysterious aspects of being human. Now, we know that the degree of introversion is biologically hardwired. Does this mean that the person we'll end up being is predetermined at birth?

This is where we'll need to separate the concepts of personality and behavior. Let me give you an example.

Let's say it's 1920. You're born into the world, screaming just like any other baby Unfortunately, your parents have internalized the ideals of the times. They scold you, and tell you that "children should be seen, not heard." You're expected to keep your mouth shut unless you're spoken to. Tough discipline is the order of the day, and when needed, it's applied with a cane. There's no room for any debate, everything basically boils down to "Father Knows Best". There's no point arguing or negotiating, even in other situations, because this is an age when being right doesn't matter as much as being older. Teachers will slap you at school for behaving in any way that even resembles defiance. You're constantly told to behave yourself, and not to run around and make noise, or otherwise act like a child. A conflict arises between the extraversion you were born with and the world you're growing up in. Society in the 1920s was very introverted, authoritarian, and ruled by tradition. The kids of today, with their "look-at-me-I-want-special-praise-just-for-taking-part" attitudes, would have seemed like aliens in those days. In this example, then, you're configured for sociable, thrill-seeking, and talkative behavior by nature. The culture around you is different, and because of this, you're likely to end up doing what many introverts do today: wear a mask. You'll adopt a more introverted behavior pattern in order to fit in and avoid isolation. Eventually, this adjustment will take root deep within you. It won't change your biology, and it'll probably never suit you too well. In other words, your behavior is a matter of how you act in a room, while your personality dictates how being in that room makes you feel. This means that you can't tell what personality somebody has just by observing them from the outside.

This issue I'm discussing here is also said to be the first and greatest question in the field of psychology: Are we mostly shaped by *nature*, or by *nurture*?

Researchers have offered different answers to this question over the years. For some time, the top psychologists believed that we're all blank slates at birth, and that the only factor influencing us is the environment that we're exposed to. After this, for a time, DNA was assumed to be the whole story. Studies of identical twins that were separated at birth have provided unique insight into these matters. Here's the most popular theory today:

The assumption is that we're formed by both nature and nurture, as well as by a third component that has only recently been considered. This is actually the most natural thing you could imagine: *free choice*. The division of influence between genetics, environment, and *choice* is presumed to be fairly even. We're all independent human beings in the sense that we can make decisions about what we want to be like. If you're extraverted, and grow up in an age where the ideals are introverted, you could still decide to say: *Hell yeah! I'm an extravert, and proud of it! I refuse to conform!*

People like Oscar Wilde and Oprah Winfrey represent successful examples of such attempts to defy both nature and nurture. They made an active decision to be the people they wanted to be, no matter what society told them. The person you end up being is the person that you've chosen to be.

Different strokes for different cultures

Some cultures are more extraverted than others. The USA is considered the most extraverted nation of all. Self-promotion is an integral part of everyday existence in their culture. Everybody learns to give a speech in first grade. Everybody practices presentation technique and rhetoric in school, regardless of whether they're introverts or extraverts. Dutch professor Geert Hofstede noted that American recruiters are likely to discount twenty percent or so of the achievements listed on a resume, just out of habit. It's simply assumed that everybody exaggerates their achievements and credentials.

The culture in Latin American countries is also very expressive. There, virtually any situation can be a social event. It can seem as though the people there live only to spend time with each other. On the other hand, certain other cultures are thought to be unusually uptight and socially restrained. This is the case with Japan and Finland, for example. A Finnish woman at my publishers told me that introversion is a national characteristic of Finns. In Finland, there's a silent agreement in place that you don't have to indulge in small talk just because you happen to be riding the elevator with somebody. Some studies suggest that our attitudes to the extraverted and introverted aspects of our own personalities change as we age. This doesn't mean that we become more of one or the other; just that many begin to explore these sides of themselves in midlife. For example, my introverted mother suddenly became interested in travel once she was past the age of fifty. The father of one of my colleagues bought his first Xbox at sixty. Most introverts cope much better with their own impending midlife than extraverts do. One study revealed that the introverted test subjects had digested this phase of their lives before it even occurred, while the extraverts tended to be taken by surprise by their own age. A classic midlife crisis, then, will generally be more of an issue for the extraverted personality types.

Summary for extraverts

✓ Extraversion is the ideal in the West, but introversion is the ideal in the East. This is why extraverted executives are more common in the West, and introverted executives are more common in the East.

✓ Introversion is biologically determined. It's a personality trait you can't change. You can train yourself to behave in a more outgoing way, but you can't do anything about your introversion.

✓ Introverts are good visualizers. We think in images, and have vivid imaginations.

Can You Make Yourself More Extraverted (and Would You Want to)?

I remember how her hand trembled against the large flip chart. She was nervous, but she spoke frankly. This was the last exercise of a management class we'd both been taking for the last few months. The point of the exercise was to write down your honest, uncensored impressions of the person sitting next to you. She told the room what she'd written about me: "He hides himself behind a shell." She looked past me nervously as she sat back down. Delivering this judgment had obviously been very difficult for her, but I wasn't hurt or offended. My immediate reaction was surprise: "Doesn't everyone?"

Since then, I've understood that this is characteristic of introverts: we're one person when we're alone, and another person in social situations. This clearly sets us apart from extraverts, who seem to carry their emotions and personalities on their sleeves.

This is also the reason why introverts are often thought to be reserved. Getting to know one of us can take a long time. This isn't just true of introverts who try to stay out of the limelight; the class clown wears a mask as well. We often remain mysteries to our loved ones.

My grandfather was a kind-hearted, stubborn, and introverted man. I lived with him for several years growing up, after my parents got divorced. He was quiet most of the time, but occasionally, he would burst into a mirthful, toothless fit of laughter. He lived alone, as his wife had passed away at quite a young age. Every day, he would walk along the beach on his own, looking at the sea. He was exceptionally handy, and lived in an enormous farmhouse that he built himself. I've never met anybody else with the same incredible degree of artistic talent that he possessed. His art lives on, and has been distributed among the members of our family. He whittled incredibly realistic wooden figurines, and made detailed model boats that he literally carved out of peeled tree trunks. He had the ability to truly see things. But he was also very reserved. I don't think he ever said a word to anybody about how he felt about his children, or his mourning process as a widower. He kept it all inside. The person I knew as my granddad was the person he chose to present to the world. Who he really was deep inside, I can't say. All I know for certain is that he loved butterscotch candy. I fully respect his choice of how to present himself to us, and I never had a problem with his formal demeanor.

Social training

Freediving is a strange pastime. The objective is to spend as long as you can under water, with just a single breath of air for company. It's quite uncomfortable at first. You can't stay under for very long. You almost panic when you start to run out of oxygen. But after a little practice, something fascinating happens: in just a short period of time, you'll increase the time you can spend diving significantly. The trick is not to struggle your way down, but to sleep your way down. Once your body has learned to relax, your experience of the ocean will be pure bliss. Also, when you do eventually feel the need to breathe, the whole thing will be a lot less stressful. Going for oxygen will be a natural impulse, that you manage without any fear or discomfort. I experience social events in much the same way. You can train your ability to hold your breath in social situations. I no longer experience discomfort when I spend time in groups, and I'm quite good at maintaining the illusion that I'm a sociable person. This is evident in the fact that people who've met me often tell me that this is how I come across. You can't do anything about your own introversion or extraversion, but you *can* train your ability to cope with different kinds of situations.

I need to clarify something about how introverts spend time with others. It's a common misconception that introverts just don't like people. The truth is that our social batteries get used up, and when this happens, it leaves us exhausted and depleted. While our batteries are still charged, we're just as sociable as any extravert. I need to confess to something I'm not proud of here: I do hate people when my batteries are flat. When this happens, a pessimism and cynicism that's far from becoming comes over me. I want to turn away from the conversation, and all of my instincts tell me to leave.

What makes my batteries run out quickly? Here are some examples:

A. Conversations in groups, in which several loud people who enjoy the sounds of their own voices participate, and nobody makes an effort to let anybody else in.
B. Getting constantly interrupted is a huge drain on my energy. Sometimes, it's obvious that the person I'm talking to isn't really listening to what I'm saying. She's just looking for openings to switch the conversation over to her own topics. This kills my batteries dead in no time.
C. Busy places where there are several conversations going on at once, where loud music is playing, and where you hear the constant clatter of dishes being washed in the background.

Our capacity for social interaction is a limited resource. That's why we don't always seek eye contact with the checkout attendants in the supermarket, and don't indulge in unnecessary small talk with the receptionist at the gym. An introverted bookworm I know put it like this: "We don't socialize with others so much as tolerate them".

We're not looking to expand our social circles every time we leave the house. Extraverts have an easier time in this sense; they have a natural knack for connecting with people they meet in the street. Our restrictive attitude to socializing means that we generally don't appreciate unannounced visits. Introverts want to be able to schedule their visits, and aren't usually waiting around in case somebody wants to talk to them about something. Unplanned visits are intrusions into our everyday lives and calendars. Unforeseen events disturb our circles. Extraverts tend to be very different in this respect. They find spontaneous visits exciting, and don't mind receiving them at any time.

The kind of social event you're at determines how relaxed the atmosphere will be. At a couples' dinner party, you all sit round a table making eye contact with each other until somebody falls asleep. This kind of social event is very demanding for an introvert, who will run out of steam by the time the appetizers are finished. At this point, having to listen to stories about vacations people took years and years ago is kind of a recipe for disaster.

Introverts like people, and need to have them around. But we prefer to spend time with others in less structured ways, that don't involve constant interaction and communication. My friend Sten got it right, I think, when he described his idea of a perfect time together: He's hanging out with some friends at his place. Two of them are on the couch, half-assedly watching some movie or other. Somebody's over by the computer, and a fourth person is in the armchair, reading a magazine. Introverts often focus on activities rather than communication when they describe rewarding social situations. Going fishing is a good example of this, as is hiking.

I remember a day and night I once spent with a childhood friend of mine. He lived abroad at the time, and we hadn't seen each other for ages. Now, he was back in Sweden for a quick visit. He arrived at my place before noon, with some sushi that he bought. I said "Hey, good to see you". He said "Hi, totally." Then, we both sat down in front of the TV, and turned my gaming console on. Before we knew it, it was the next morning; we'd been up all night playing games. You could fit a transcript of the entire dialog between the two of us that night on the back of a stamp. But we still both felt that we'd gotten some quality time in, and we both had fun.

Introverts stockpile social energy for situations where they need it. Too much socializing overloads our brain circuitry, and makes it difficult for us to have a good time.

> *Guiltroversion; the guilt from wanting to see no one and do nothing; to want to be completely alone and feel all your feeling, especially when you don't have the energy to explain to another person.*
> (Source: The Emotionary)

Teen angst

Many introverts feel maladjusted and irritable during the stage of life when everybody is their most out of place: *puberty*. The teen years are pretty much the definition of angst to begin with, and the challenge of fitting in and acting normal while hormones wage war within us and every day is like a song by the Cure is no mean feat. Being uncomfortable in social situations only makes things worse. To top it off, introverts are pronounced individualists, which often means that groups will perceive them as odd, because they're not very meticulous about observing fashion trends and other important social markers.

This means that most introverts spend their teen years running a long gauntlet of embarrassing moments. We get the earring done in the wrong ear, or choose a brand of clothes that's actually associated with a different subculture than the one we want to belong to.

Studies have shown that extraverts generally have better

self-esteem growing up. Perhaps this has something to do with how the media portrays introverted personalities? In the movies, the teen introvert is often a geeky math wiz with braces, who keeps getting pushed around by extraverts. *Ferris Bueller's Day Off* is a classic example of this. Matthew Broderick's fast-talking character spends the whole movie convincing his introverted friend to do things he doesn't want to do, including borrowing his father's prized vintage Ferrari, which ends up getting totaled. The teen years are a tough time for introverts, partly because of their lack of suitable role models. Many of them make up for it later on, because something happens to them after all of those teenage mishaps.

Introverts mature differently from extraverts. All that internal processing of thoughts and emotions they do over the years helps them grow. The introvert might still be quiet, uptight and socially restrained, this is hardwired after all, but as the years go by, a natural stability develops, which gives them great integrity. Of course, this isn't universally true, but many older introverts have both their feet firmly planted on the ground. This is simply due to the fact that spending all that time brooding and contemplating your own inner being will eventually give you a pretty good understanding of yourself, and understanding tends to bring acceptance. Introverts are quick to accept themselves, as well as their strengths and weaknesses.

Happiness

Studies have shown that as a rule, extraverts are happier than introverts. To quote a Swedish comedian: "Happy people are just people who don't know any better". Suicide is slightly more common among introverts. You could interpret this as meaning that the positive attitudes of extraverts actually help them achieve success in life, but that's not quite correct.

If you're successful, people will tend to believe that you're an extravert. They'd be surprised to hear you refer to yourself as an introvert. In the West, we associate successful behavior with extraversion. Successful behavior includes constant networking, belief in one's own ability, openness, good verbal skills, competitive spirit, and so on.

In the East, introversion is the norm. There, reflection, thoughtfulness, and dignity are held in high esteem. Speaking first, or loudest, is frowned upon. Standing out from the crowd is a bad thing. This sentiment is expressed in Japanese proverbs, such as "The nail that sticks out will be hammered." This is why introverts are the happiest people in these cultures. So, it seems that happiness is actually connected to the ideals of your society instead, and to how close to this ideal your own personality happens to be. There are often religious reasons for why some ideal or other becomes predominant in a certain area. In the East, Buddhism is a powerful factor in favor of the introverted ideal.

This ideal also has a great impact on executive roles. In the West, we favor extraverted executives, while South Korean business is dominated by introverts. Sweden is unusually extraverted in this respect, and it's estimated that less than a quarter of our executives are introverts.

I like thought experiments. Something I've been enjoying lately is asking people about the "Last Human on Earth" scenario. The question I ask them is this: "You wake up one morning. All of the people and animals on earth are gone. Everything else is still there. What do you do?"

It seems to me that people answer this question differently based on their preferences. Introverts might answer that they would grow plants, read books, and learn to play musical instruments. One introvert told me he would start collecting luxury cars. However, extraverts' responses tend to be something along the lines of "I'd find a Porsche and drive it into a brick wall." I've heard lots of creative ways to commit suicide since I began asking people this question.

Extraverts seem to live to spend time with other people, while introverts think there could be meaningful things to do even in an uninhabited world.

Do you rule the bar, or do you rule the mind?

Extraverts are social beings, who can feel exhilarated and euphoric in situations involving many people. They have a kind of passion, or glow, that makes them the life of the party, and they're always the ones who close the bar. Introverts know how to party as well, but we enjoy the earlier parts of the evening more than the later ones. It's never made sense to me when people want to stop having drinks at somebody's place to "go out." "Why should we go to a place where we have to stand in line to get in, pay a cover charge, and then spend the rest of the night yelling over the loudspeakers?" The energy of an extravert can seem infectious and invigorating, although mainly to other extraverts. They can be self-centered. I've met extraverts who refer to themselves in the third person. But most extraverts are friendly people, who do their part to brighten everybody's mood. They love other people, and they love sharing their lives and their happiness with them. The charm of an extravert can often be mistaken for flirtation, even when they intend nothing of the sort. It's not rare for them to have a knack for coaxing introverts out of our shells and forcing us to have fun. They tend to influence other people, and sometimes even dominate them. At parties, they often make it their mission to loosen everybody up, especially the introverts by the bar. It's always an extravert who bounces over to drag an introvert onto the dance floor. Personally, I hate being chased onto a dance floor. At parties, I feel like one of those lobsters they keep in fish tanks in restaurants; it's only a matter of time before somebody singles me out to be eaten.

Gifts

A lot of research has been done to investigate the ways in which the brains of introverts and extraverts process information. Extraverts are quick thinkers, and have the edge on introverts when it comes to sensory input. Extraverts keep the part of the brain that processes visual impressions running in high gear. If I were to ask you to name a fruit that begins with the letter P, you're likely to respond faster if you're an extravert.

But when it comes to other kinds of tasks, which require deeper and more persistent thought, introverts make up the ground they've lost in no time. We think slowly, but in larger steps. We absorb a lot of information in a single thought process, before finishing our analysis. You could compare it to filling up a whole truck with thoughts before transporting them to our mouths, or pens. Extraverts use a messenger bike instead, which is quick to get going, and can make several runs back and forth in the same amount of time. There's a big difference between being stupid and thinking slowly. The latter is a characteristic of introverts which is often mistaken for the former. Being the first person to talk about a problem is in no way related to being the person who actually solves it.

The vast majority of musical prodigies are introverts. There's a logic to this, if you consider what's involved in the process of becoming an expert in any field. The road to true expertise is paved with a horrendous amount of monotonous repetition. It's all about maintaining sharp focus and deep commitment. These are characteristics which are closely aligned with the introverted aspects of the human personality. Introverts don't get fatigued by these tasks as easily as extraverts do, and this is why they can sometimes possess highly specialized skill sets. Introversion is one of the most dominant attributes of truly gifted people. A statistical observation which supports this is that the higher a person's IQ is, the greater the probability is that this person has an introverted personality. Mensa claims that the majority of their members are introverts. Emotional intelligence, or EQ, is also a strong suit of introverts. This might seem strange. How can it be that socially awkward and introverted people are good at understanding emotions? It's been claimed that introversion can be regarded as a kind of social dyslexia. This simply isn't true; we're very good at decoding social situations. This is assumed to be explained by the fact that introverts observe rather than participate. We take note of and analyze the reactions and behaviors of others, as well as our own. The standard issue kit for introverts includes a small on-board psychologist, who observes and ponders everything around us. The ability to stick with a task for an extended period of time, and give it deep focus without getting bored, is correlated with a high IQ. Without any doubt, this is the single trait that's been the most useful to me in life. Without stubbornness and repetition, I would never have gotten anywhere.

This has become my standard recipe for success. When I start out learning something, my performance is average or below average; I'm never one of the best at that point. Energetic extraverts are usually the ones who get going the fastest with new activities. But in time, through sheer stubbornness, I'll often end up overtaking the others, who have begun to lose interest, and have lowered their ambitions along the way. Both aspects have their own strengths and weaknesses.

One of my more extraverted acquaintances once told me how challenging it is for him to read a book. He claims that for each page he reads, he has to overcome about twenty distractions. Trains of thought and impressions come at him from all directions, snatching his attention away. The extraverted intellect is very active, constantly feeling out each impulse and impression in its surroundings.

On a few occasions, I've had extraverts who wanted start working out tag along to the gym with me. I've exercised regularly for the last twenty years. It gives me peace, but it's not exactly inspiring. Strength training is an extremely monotonous activity, and yields a pretty low payoff in terms of results. If you're really ambitious, you can expect to put on about two pounds of muscle in a year. However, achieving this weight gain requires a strong dedication to maintaining your diet, to training the right way, and, most importantly, to training regularly. It's not a particularly social form of exercise, either. The effort required for these slow gains means that few extraverts find going to the gym very inspiring in the long term, which is my experience exactly. My extraverted friends have started out full of energy, and taken their training very seriously for a month or so. But because the results take time, they've tended to grow tired of it after that. Monotony and introversion are a perfect match. A dominant proportion of elite athletes in individual sports are introverts. It's my hypothesis that the reason for this is their tolerance for monotony. On the other hand, team sports seem to be rife with outgoing personalities. Team spirit is generally a stronger drive in extraverts than it is in introverts, who don't really feel like they're part of the team anyway. Introverted stars often have a reputation for being boring or arrogant. Introverts aren't naturally friendly to people who approach them out of the blue in supermarkets, and they often find themselves at odds with the press.

For the very same reason, I suspect this book would never have been written if its author was more sociable. If that had been the case, I would have spent my time drinking rosé wine and discussing politics with loose acquaintances on the porch instead.

It's doubtless that much of what we think of as talent is the result of an extreme amount of repetition. It takes incredible discipline to go to the soccer field for practice when your feet are covered with blisters and the rain is pouring down. It takes oceans of patience to make your way through all of the reading you need to get done along the way to a professorship. This discipline, and this patience, are both hallmarks of the introverted personality.

An introvert's wish list

Here are some words of advice for people who want to live in harmony with the introverted ecosystem.

1. Avoid unannounced house calls. Don't just show up at the front door. Call first, or preferably text, to ask if it's a good time to come over.
2. Keep things brief on the phone. Most messages of any value can be communicated in three sentences or less. Have a reason for calling. If we don't answer, feel free to leave a message.
3. Spell properly. Don't use CAPITAL LETTERS for no reason - we'll think you're yelling at us! Don't use thousands of exclamation marks, it makes you seem childish.
4. Don't force spontaneous decisions in one sitting. Rational decision making takes time. Provide the relevant information before the decisions need to be made, and leave us alone to think.
5. Avoid intense eye contact.
6. Leave space in conversations. Silence is not some hole that needs filling.
7. Let us finish what we're saying.
8. Don't disturb us when we're concentrating. It takes us a long time to get back to wherever we were before we were interrupted.
9. Don't speak loudly on your mobile phone in places where people can't easily get away from you.

Summary for extraverts

✓ Introverts dominate the literary, technological, and artistic domains. However, we're the minority in rock music and politics.

✓ Introverted people have an unbreakable discipline when it comes to performing repetitive tasks that yield slow progress. Classical musicians are usually introverts, for this very reason.

✓ The higher a person's IQ is, the more likely this person is to be an introvert. Most of Mensa's members are introverts.

Do Extraverts Have the Gift of the Gab?

The impromptu speech

I heard my name being announced. Hundreds of happy faces turned to me, and hundreds of glasses were raised. This warm evening in Barcelona had suddenly become even warmer. Deafening applause broke out. I was caught off guard. My heart was racing, and my legs were trembling. "Say something!" the MC said, and handed me the microphone. I held it tightly, with whitening knuckles, and withdrew into total passivity. All I was able produce was a strange guttural hum. This was followed by the longest awkward silence in history. The audience applauded dutifully as I returned to my seat. I felt like it was all happening to somebody else.

Winston Churchill once said: "An impromptu speech takes three weeks to prepare." This statement sounds very much like something an introvert would say. Having to speak without advance preparation is not our idea of fun at all. When an introvert gives an impromptu speech, what you're hearing is actually a series of monologues and punchlines that they've learned in the past. Introversion entails the need to think things through. We need to choose our words inside our heads before we're ready to share them with the world. As I mentioned earlier, there are countless examples of successful introverted speakers. Those people created roles for themselves as speakers. Nobody would have expected that the nervous up-and-comer who froze on that stage in Barcelona would become a renowned speaker one day.

You can't tell if people are introverts or not just by looking at them. Of course, there are a few visual characteristics that are considered typical of introverts. I could mention things like conservative dress in earthy colors, or gray, or black.

Restrained facial expressions and a monotonous tone of voice are other classic signs. However, many people have simply been influenced by the current zeitgeist. Many have been taught rhetoric in school, and have learned to develop their own images. Perhaps they've intentionally given themselves an image which ensures that they'll be noticed. For this reason, many of the classical signs are no longer reliable. The thing that reveals a particular person's attitude is his or her overall behavior. The important question is "What do you do when you're free to do anything you like?" The answer to that question will reveal all. True introverts spend a lot of quality time with themselves.

I have a good friend named Rasmus, who orchestrates situations to make himself the center of attention. He considers himself an introvert, but that's not what anybody else would think. He calls it his "onstage persona." He can play the role of a self-assured party host whenever he needs to. With a steady voice, and proud posture, he walks on stage, and to all appearances, he speaks directly from the heart. But he always has a concealed note full of prompters with him, and he always makes sure to get some time alone before show time. He plays a part, and he does it very well.

I've become aware of this since it began to be discussed in the media. Many of the people we regard as extraverts are really nothing of the sort. They've made a habit of avoiding social contexts to find peace ever since they were children. They may never have understood that they were actually introverts, and wondered if there was something wrong with them instead.

Spontaneity and stress are a dangerous combination for me. On the same night that I gave that "speech" in Barcelona, I managed to tell our corporate director that "only a man knows how to please a man." To this day, I can't really explain why I said that. I was under pressure, and felt like I had to come up with something funny and unforgettable to say. In retrospect, given those criteria, I'd have to say I succeeded at the task. I take some comfort in the fact that

I'm far from the only person who's prone to saying stupid things under duress. Nobody could possibly be dumber than a stressed introvert. Studies have shown that introverts have rather sensitive thought processes. Stress can jumble up our thoughts. Our usual strengths (logic, reflection, and analysis) are suddenly nowhere to be found. Extraverts, on the other hand, tend to be pushed to perform better when they're subjected to stress and pressure. They work faster with their backs to the wall, and are able to maintain their precision despite this. Some extraverts claim that their greatest achievements in life have come in the heat of battle. Stress is the Achilles' heel of introverts. We're at our best when the chips *aren't* down.

If I'd been given some advance warning that I was about to win an award, I could have given a much better "impromptu" speech. The strengths of introverts rely on advance planning, reflection, and preparation. My first question whenever I'm asked to do something is always "How long do I have to think about it?". Introverts need to have some distance to the issue they're considering.

Could an introvert become just as good a speaker as an enormously outgoing extravert? Instinctively, the answer to this seems to be no. The stereotypical speaker is a vibrant extravert, who races onto the stage like a comet. Howling bundles of energy like Steve Ballmer at Microsoft have become iconic. In a video on YouTube, which has since become a legendary online meme, he runs onto the stage, dripping with sweat, and screams: "I LOOOVE THIS COOMPANNNYYY YEAAHHHH!" The whirlwind phenom Clifford Stoll was given the TED Speaker of the year award in 2010. These two have both become archetypal of the *inspirational speaker*.

At first sight, the great speakers of our time all seem to be extraverts – some of them are even borderline manic! There are plenty of great speakers who have obvious extraverted personality traits, and much of the expressive body language that's typical of extraversion is also associated with the concept of charisma. In the 1960s, an experiment was performed by a gentleman who called himself Dr. Fox. Dr. Fox, who was really an actor, went on a tour of different schools all over the USA, and delivered speeches to the students. Dr. Fox was incredibly charismatic, and communicated his message with great energy. With a racing pulse and intense body language, he captivated the high school students in the audience. Afterwards, they were filled with enthusiasm, and felt that they'd learned a lot, despite the fact that they didn't remember a single thing he'd said. The point of the experiment was that what Dr. Fox said was really just nonsense. His whole presentation was riddled with logical flaws. The conclusion drawn from these experiments was this: if a speaker is sufficiently charismatic, he or she will be regarded as an authority figure, regardless of what's actually being said. Charisma trumps content, at least in the short term. That's why the stereotypical image of a speaker is so clearly extraverted.

Are introverted speakers simply suckers for punishment?

But if all this is true, how can it be that some of the most powerful speakers around are so quiet in their private lives? How was an introverted man able to speak up and make his dream of a color-blind society heard all over the world, where it's still echoing today, sixty years later? "I have a dream" has been called the most powerful speech in history. I still get goose bumps whenever I hear that fuzzy recording of Martin Luther King's words. He sings his message, and his voice trembles with its power.

Susan Cain, Al Gore, and Emma Watson are all introverts, but they've all delivered very powerful speeches. How is it that many introverts are such good lecturers, when you would expect the opposite based on their social preference?

The perfect speech

Dale Carnegie has been dubbed the father of modern public speaking. He claimed that any truly effective speech depends on three factors, none of which has anything to do with the speaker's level of comfort in the speaking situation.

1. Don't reveal more than the tip of the iceberg of your total knowledge. If you're asked to speak about a topic for five minutes, you should have sufficient knowledge to speak about it for fifty minutes.

2. The audience needs to feel that you've *earned* the right to speak about your topic. They need to sense that you've worked hard, and shown great discipline, to become an expert in the field. For example, any holocaust survivor would have much more credibility regarding that particular topic than I could ever have.

3. The third component, and perhaps the most important one, is passion. You need to have that geeky, obsessive fire that makes your speech genuinely passionate. Enthusiasm is contagious in a speaker; it causes her to give off signals that attract the interest of others. When we hear her speak, we think: I want that too, I want to feel that passion!

These three components come naturally to introverts. The fact that we're so uncomfortable with the actual speaking situation means that we're likely to study up more than we actually need to in preparing for our presentations. When an introvert stands up to speak, she'll often be light years beyond the point of being entitled to speak on the topic. She'll already have rehearsed and practiced her speech many times in front of the mirror. In all likelihood, her loved ones have already served as a test audience, and offered their critiques of the presentation. We prepare meticulously, and hope that others will do the same. Introversion gives you a great sense of respect for the spoken word. When you see an introvert take the stage of his or her own free will, you can be certain that this person is genuinely passionate about the topic.

In my experience, extraverts often seem to take their appearances much more lightly. They apply the finishing touches to their PowerPoint presentations while the audience takes their seats. They begin speaking without knowing where they'll end up, but they're backed up by their optimism and their conviction that it'll all work out for the best. Speaking comes naturally to them.

On several occasions, I've had the opportunity to compare my own style with that of other people, who are much more extraverted or introverted than myself. Here are some of the things I've noticed:

Extraverted speakers...

- ✓ Captivate the audience with their force of personality.
- ✓ Challenge and activate the audience in the purely social sense. Don't mind touching their audiences, and try to form relationships with them.
- ✓ Often include playful activities for the audience to participate in. Encourage their listeners to make physical contact with strangers in the room. Also encourage discussing things in pairs, or making eye contact with other audience members. I don't think I need to tell you how introverted audience members feel about this kind of thing.
- ✓ Change their material from one time to the next. Say different things on different occasions, to keep their message fresh. Changing things up means that the speaker has to stay alert.
- ✓ Pay less attention to detail, and more attention to building energy.

- ✓ Strive to establish dialog, or at least the illusion of dialog, throughout their presentation.
- ✓ Tend to have a little less in the way of formal knowledge, but more in the way of vibrant and dynamic personalities. Spend more time on presentation than on content.
- ✓ Experience an adrenaline rush before beginning their speech, rather than nerves.
- ✓ Are excessively wasteful with time. Enjoy speaking so much that they tend to go over their allotted time.
- ✓ Base the highlight moments of their lectures on the audience's sense of recognition.
- ✓ Respond to every question from the audience, regardless of whether they know the answer or not.
- ✓ Will often use content that is personal in nature, and full of situations they've experienced firsthand. They try to communicate emotions, and don't mind opening up to their audience.
- ✓ Often speak about themselves to a great extent, and usually begin their presentations with a PowerPoint slide with their bio.

Introverted speakers...

- ✓ Captivate the audience with their message.
- ✓ Use intricate ideas and unexpected points to challenge their audiences' intellects.
- ✓ Have a meticulous approach, and improve on the same core material continuously.
- ✓ Memorize large chunks of information, and put more effort into content than into presentation.
- ✓ Focus on perfecting their lectures.
- ✓ Appear to be improvising, even when they're not.
- ✓ Often have understated body language. Steve Jobs' famous speech at Princeton is an excellent example of how a speaker can spellbind an audience without using facial gestures or audience interaction.
- ✓ Design the whole package as a script.

✓ Have butterflies in their stomach when show time draws near.

✓ Base the highlight moments of their lectures on ingenious theories, relevant contexts, and solid arguments.

✓ Don't consider it a matter of prestige to appear to know everything. Are prepared to admit it when they don't know the answer to a question from the audience.

✓ Often speak about interesting and inspiring topics, without any great emphasis on their own experiences, and maintain their distance and integrity throughout the presentation.

✓ Focus on the topic at hand in their speeches.

The problem with having a good poker face

One of the dangers introverts face is what happens when we find a topic particularly interesting. When we're truly interested in something, we can look as lively as a chunk of frozen fish stew. The deader our gaze, and the less emotion our faces reveal, the more intensely we're listening. An empty expression on the outside is a sign of great activity on the inside. This contrasts with extraverts, who function the opposite way. Their facial gestures grow livelier as their interest increases. My wife has instructed me to utter a syllable now and then while she's speaking, mostly because she's worried that people around us will think that she's some crazy person who's talking to herself if I don't.

This has caused me some consternation during several of my lecturing appearances. Even though I'm an introvert myself, I sometimes forget what this poker face means. I think most introverts never realize this. Sometimes, I've felt that the audience wasn't giving me anything back. The seats have been packed with vacant faces, which even looked annoyed to me. But afterwards, the same people have approached me to tell me how captivated they were by my presentation. Introverts simply signal their interest differently than extraverts do.

Analogous communications issues exist within the animal kingdom. For example, when a dog wags its tail, it's happy, but when a cat does the same thing, it wants to kill you. This is one of the reasons why cats and dogs don't always get along. I make a point of trying to be more active when I'm listening to people. When I'm focusing on listening, my gaze tends to shift away. I have an easier time concentrating on what's being said when I don't also have to process visual impressions of the speaker. Sometimes, closing my eyes while I listen can help. This is because of the many images that are produced in my mind when I listen. I find it too distracting to have to keep track of two cinema screens at once. I can understand how people could mistake this for a lack of interest. Nowadays, I try to signal interest by leaning forward, nodding knowingly, and laughing when somebody says something funny. Sometimes, my daydreaming gets the better of me, and lands me in trouble. In those situations, I'll only be half-listening, and I often end up laughing at the wrong moment. Some people communicate with great intensity. They speak quickly, and loudly. They lay claim to every last second of silence, and they look you right in the eye when they speak. These are common extraverted traits, but I know a few introverts who also dive into conversations this way. The effect that this has on introverts, myself included, is to cause us to turn away to an angle of about forty-five degrees, to shield ourselves from their torrent of words. My wife has coined the phrase "the iPhone bubble". That's her term for the defense mechanism I use in these situations. When somebody gets too intense, I lower my gaze, and check my phone. This gives me a few seconds of rest from stimuli, so that I can catch my breath. Our conventional ideas about speakers and audiences are simply wrong. We *think* we want to listen to extraverted speakers, and we *think* we want to speak to introverted audiences. In reality, it's often the other way round. You want an extraverted audience, because they'll immerse themselves, take an interest, and get inspired in ways that can electrify the whole room. An introverted speaker makes sure to get to the point in a timely fashion rather than wandering off on an improvised odyssey of words. An introverted audience will be restrained, and will sometimes voice criticism over minor factual inaccuracies: "According to Wikipedia, importing avocados to New Zealand wasn't allowed until 1979 – not 1978, like you said!"

Fake smiles

People who know me well have told me that I tense up when I'm lecturing. For some reason, I'm prone to getting a bad case of *resting bitch face*. I've tried smiling more, but I've come to the realization that my lack of expression is caused by my strong internal focus: the more I smile, the harder it is for me to remember what to say. For some reason, smiling puts me off track. My poker face is a fixed aspect of how I function, which I share with many other introverts.

I'd even claim that this poker face is one of the *perks* of introversion. I remember being very nervous during some of the lectures I've given. My voice was unsteady, and I felt my cheeks throb from blushing so hard. I was wet with sweat, and my lips stuck together. But afterwards, I was told that I projected great calm and assuredness, despite having been so nervous. In a lecturing situation, knowing that your nerves won't show is a source of strength.

One of the main reasons why introverts can be so comfortable in the role of a lecturer is that it gives us a chance to speak about something without being interrupted. In everyday conversation, we're used to having extraverts decide that it's their turn to speak the instant we pause for a moment. Once you're on stage, you get to communicate your content in the exact way you desire to. On top of this, you get to deliver it all in one go. In many ways, the role of a speaker is ideal for any introvert who's able to conquer her stage fright.

Speaking is silver, but silence is golden

Our chairs were set out in a circle. The organizer was obviously an extravert. No matter which way I turned, I'd have to face someone else's inquiring gaze. And so, a few of us were busy examining our shoes instead. The more outgoing participants looked straight ahead, mirroring the smiles they faced across the room. I noticed her right away. Her appearance screamed "Look at me!" Her leopard print tights, bright red spectacle frames, and colorful feather boa were pretty eye-catching. We began with the standard "stand up and introduce yourself" exercise. Or, as introverts experience it: "Brag as much about yourself as you can in a short time." Everybody takes turns standing up to speak. For each person who does it, the pressure mounts a little more for the next speaker. Every time the turn is passed to somebody new, it becomes just a little bit more important to present yourself as funny, credible, successful, and sophisticated. I understand the purpose of this exercise. The lady in the loud outfit couldn't keep still. She was too impatient to get to tell us all who she was. Her acrylic nails, which were decorated with stars, were beating out an impatient rhythm against her armrest. She didn't hear a single word of what anybody else was saying. Eventually, her turn came. She stepped into the middle of the circle, and, underlining her statements with loud gestures, began to tell us about her greatest passion in life: herself. "The first thing you'll notice about me is that I like to be the center of attention. I like talking a lot, and fortunately, I have the gift of the gab."

She didn't stop there. At a pace of about a million words a minute, she launched into a monolog that lasted for fifteen minutes. I was so astonished by her egotism that my eyebrows began to get sore. This was pure narcissism. She was pretty much a caricature of a high-grade extravert.

Speaking doesn't come naturally to anybody. Many extraverts have the gift of the gab, as this lady put it. But far fewer of them actually speak *well*. The fact that you have an easy time standing up to give an impromptu speech doesn't necessarily mean that you're any good at it. The greatest challenge for an introverted speaker is to find the courage to do it. Even after the countless lectures I've given, I always have butterflies in my stomach before my speaking appearances. The challenge for an extravert is rather to cut down on their words. An inexperienced extraverted speaker is likely to use too many words, and too few pauses. I had to undergo a week of torturous speaking classes at the Dale Carnegie Institute before I could begin my journey. These were long days, full of exercises in which I had to give unprepared lectures on various topics. My voice and my hands trembled throughout every presentation. I came home each night drenched in sweat, with my eyes glazed over. The training exhausted me mentally. But I kept with it, because I could sense that this was something I could get good at. After that week I was up and running, and I've simply kept going from there. I'm convinced that anybody could give a lecture. It all comes down to practice and being self-critical. I've found that putting great emphasis on the first sentence that I utter is key for me. I take great care to choose the right one-liner or insightful quote. Then, I use it to break the ice with my audience. When I'm Stockholm, for example, I tend to begin by apologizing for my speech impediment, i.e., my Skåne accent. Once the audience has laughed, the ice has been broken, and my nerves will have settled. It seems to me that nervous tension is a constant companion of any introvert in this kind of situation. Stage fright is simply something you have to learn to deal with. It's caused by hormones. It doesn't take much to stress an introvert out. Even though I've lectured several hundred times, it still makes me uncomfortable at times. Now, I'm a good speaker not *despite* my introversion, but *because of it.*

Summary for extraverts

✓ The respect an introvert has for the spoken word becomes a strength in the role of a speaker. An introverted speaker will tend to be well-prepared, knowledgeable, and good at sticking to the time limit.

✓ An introvert can definitely take center-stage in social contexts, for example, in the role of a speaker. However, they need some time to charge their batteries between appearances.

✓ When an introverted person listens intently, he or she can appear to be in a catatonic state of shock.

Meaningful Encounters

Introverts would have an easier time talking to extraverts if it weren't for the sheer quantity of words they use. A pronounced extravert doesn't look to eliminate words; instead, he'll look to fill every last bit of silence with longer sentences, without trying very hard to be concise and to the point. Getting to finish your train of thought isn't an obvious priority for somebody who thinks of conversation as an end in itself. This is one of the most common problems that arise when extraverts and introverts enter into dialog with each other. Another potential source of irritation is the difference in how they take turns speaking. An extravert will interrupt others when he or she feels like it (just think of Donald Trump), and will expect others to interrupt him or her right back. Interrupting others, and being interrupted back, are both natural aspects of the flow of conversation between two extraverts.

Introverts behave quite differently. I get annoyed when somebody interrupts me or shouts me down if I spend too long choosing the right words to use. Phone calls are a pain, because you can't see the person on the other end. The logical way to get your say in a phone conversation is simply to interrupt the other party. I know many people feel like I don't care about them because I don't call them often enough. But the fact is that I hate using the phone, and that's really all there is to it. Many introverts share this sense of guilt over their phone-o-phobia.

I hate having my sentences completed for me even more than I hate being interrupted. It makes my blood boil. An introvert's idea of a good dialog follows the same general pattern as meaningful work; that is, it occurs in sequence. When I get interrupted, my natural inclination is to fall silent rather than repeat myself. A dislike for having to repeat yourself is a common feature among introverts. To quote a somewhat inebriated gentleman who was having an argument with a nightclub bouncer: "Shut up when you're talking to me!"

Extravert communication – one part substance, seven parts words

If you're an extravert, eighty percent of your words are likely to be inessential. To an introvert, the power of communication resides in the silence *between* the words. Being able to communicate something within the bounds of the other party's attention span is the whole secret here. In our house, we've established what we call the *three sentence rule*. The point of this is to ensure that I'll catch what Hanna is saying when she has something important to communicate.

Stated simply, the rule is that you should always be able to summarize the point you're making in three sentences or less. If the message is longer than that, my attention span might not be up to the task, and there's a chance that I'll begin daydreaming about unicorns. One of the challenges extraverts pose to introverts has to do with how they hide the substance of what they're saying behind a wall of words. They tuck the really important stuff away in some parallel train of thought or other. This means that my thoughts will be bouncing back and forth all over the story I'm being told, and I won't be able to take in any of the content.

"And then I told Linda that she'd better think about how - WOW! Did you see that? An elk! Anyway, there's no way I'm going to be her secretary, and ... by the way, she's having a party after work on the 5th. What do you think I should wear to it? And *could you pick the kids up that day*? I've never seen an elk up close like that before. Yikes, I'm getting really hungry! Not burgers, we eat that all the time, and it sucks that I've put on so much weight – no more candy for me after this weekend, OK? Linda has lost so much weight; she looks almost unhealthy."

That's pretty representative of how a conversation with my extraverted wife can go. If I also happen to be driving while we're talking, it's difficult for me to remember the task she gave me in the middle of all that.

"You didn't pick the kids up? But we agreed that you would!"

Missing parts of a conversation in this way doesn't mean that you have a bad attitude, it simply means that you have an agile mind. Earlier, I described how extraverts often flit around like butterflies in social situations. An introvert's mind moves in a similar fashion.

I mentioned the three sentence rule when I was interviewed about introversion for the Swedish newspaper Svenska Dagbladet. I've been told that a CEO who read about it introduced the rule at his company. I'd like to raise a warning here, because Hanna has found a loophole: really long sentences.

Mistaking enthusiasm for apathy

Enthusiasm can cause difficulties in relationships. This becomes clear when you show something to an extravert and ask for their opinion. It's as though the opinion was already present in the extravert's mind before you even asked. Usually, you'll get a long stream of thoughts and commentary right away. Their judgment is put into words the very millisecond they conceptualize it. This makes extraverts great people to test your ideas on. It's as though you got to listen to their brains while they think. Extraverts are good at putting their impressions into words.

However, when introverts are asked for feedback, problems will often arise.

"What do you think about this contrast wallpaper I found online?" I lean my head to one side and squint. I try to visualize the short side of the room with that wallpaper. This reflection takes me a few seconds. In the meantime, Hanna has gotten annoyed, and hisses: "OK! I guess you didn't like that one!" Silence is interpreted as something negative. I've experienced this several times in my professional life as well. An extravert takes an introvert's careful reflection as pessimism. In this case, I'd say that the people who need to adjust their behavior are the extraverts. My advice to them is to wait for an opinion before they make their minds up about what introverts are thinking. We react more slowly, and our thought processes are different. We choose our words after we think, not while we're thinking.

There's a big difference between being stupid and taking your time. An introvert's thoughts move slowly, but they go deep.

My greatest achievements at work have all followed the same simple process: challenge me, then give me time to think. After that, I'll deliver something good. If I have to sum up an issue and present a solution to it right away, in the meeting where it first came up, my performance will tend to be quite poor.

Silence

It's an obvious fact that many extraverts get uncomfortable when conversations run out of steam. They begin to get anxious after a few seconds of silence. In this situation, they'll often repeat something that's already been discussed. Hanna has told me about one of the conclusions she's drawn from her experience of recruiting.

She claims that extraverts have an easy time speaking naturally without advance preparation. They tend to have a lot of confidence in their verbal skills. She feels that introverted candidates perform well in most interview situations. They stick to answering the question, and don't keep making little brain farts all the time. What I'm referring to as brain farts here are those unnecessary conversation fillers people use, such as "like" or "ummmm". She remembers a young, bouncy guy who finished all of his sentences with a confident "knowwhatimsayin?" He *didn't* get the job.

People who spend a lot of time around introverts would do well to learn to appreciate the pauses that arise in conversations, and make friends with the silence. A classmate of mine once said that the best evidence of a strong friendship is that you're not bothered by silences.

Although Hanna appreciates the thoughtfulness of introverts in recruiting contexts, there are many situations where it's quite inappropriate. We live in a world that moves quickly, where the right sequence of words can dictate the outcome of any situation. This gives people with quick tongues an edge. We're encouraged to climb over each other to get ahead in line, especially when we're applying for a job. Job seeking coaches tell people to call the recruiter even if the ad says that they don't have time to take phone calls. It's a way of showing interest. This extraverted norm is especially obvious in classrooms and in work meetings. The importance of *speaking up* is often emphasized. Many people interpret this as meaning that you should *speak over* others. An introvert's desire to reflect and slowly massage the right sequence of words into existence isn't particularly well suited for the everyday struggles we encounter at work.

Opinions differ on what constitutes a rewarding exchange. I'm occasionally contacted by extraverts who claim to want to access my expertise. I always aim to please, so I keep walking into this trap over and over. When we actually meet, they'll sometimes speak non-stop for the duration of the meeting, until we run out of time. "Thanks, you've given me so much to think about," she says as we're finishing up. I can never make sense of that, because the extravert seems to genuinely think that we've had a real exchange.

103

Integrity

I'm a bona fide movie buff. I read online articles about upcoming movies with great interest. I've noticed how people on movie forums tend to discuss movie stars, and categorize them as "down-to-earth folk" or "people who have let their celebrity get to their heads." Stars are categorically divided into *good people* and *arrogant assholes*. Generally speaking, a star who takes the time to sign autographs whenever he or she is asked to will be considered one of the good guys, while stars who aren't OK with being approached by fans in ski lifts are judged to be full of themselves.

I don't see it that way. I'm convinced that this is yet another case where it all comes down to extraversion and introversion. Bill Clinton has been described as the most extraverted human being in the universe. I've read descriptions of how crowds energize him, and how he gets more and more energetic the more people he meets. People like Bill have good reputations for always having time for people. This is hardly strange, considering that extraversion is basically the drive to meet new people. A star like Tobey Maguire, on the other hand, has the opposite reputation. He gets uncomfortable when fans try to start conversations with him in the street, and withdraws from encounters of this kind. Because of this, he gets crucified in the forums, and labeled an *arrogant asshole*. I can understand that it would be annoying to have people constantly interrupt you when you're trying to enjoy some quality time with your loved ones in a restaurant. Tobey's great commitment to a number of different charitable causes doesn't seem to attract the same kind of attention. Let's be clear: what determines whether or not you're a good person isn't how prepared you are to talk to strangers at the drop of a hat. That's just a measure of is how outgoing you are.

How would *you* react if you were suddenly approached by one of your customers in the middle of a picnic with your family? Suppose she began to discuss a matter with you that you should clearly be handled during working hours, without showing any respect for your private time. It seems to me that all these supposedly arrogant stars might just as well be introverts who also happen to have a great degree of personal integrity.

I can remember sharing cubicles with some incredibly intelligent introverted coworkers. The people we're talking about here have an almost ridiculous ability to solve logical problems, but haven't managed to grasp basic courtesies like saying *hello*, *thank you*, or *good morning*. Extraversion and introversion are never an excuse for disrespecting people.

Inside the bubble

Introverts can be almost religious about their personal space. Studies have shown that introverts and extraverts both prefer to keep the same distance to people who they're speaking to. However, introverts are much more sensitive to invasions. We get uncomfortable when people get too close. Standing in a packed elevator is agony for me. Generally speaking, introverts seem to value the concept of privacy much more.

We're allergic to aggressive sales tactics. We find those guys with slicked back hair who pitch mobile phone plans to passers-by in malls particularly annoying. Sometimes, we can feel like we're running some kind of gauntlet through the stores while the sales staff tries to attach themselves to us like leeches.

The contemporary sales approach is generally based on making eye contact and addressing people in a loud tone of voice that suggests you already know the other person: "Well howdy there!"

That technique is great, assuming the intent is to make certain you'll *never* close a sale with one of us. A fun thing to do in these situations is to reply in the same exact tone of voice: "Hiiiii!" This immediately makes it plain how fake the whole interaction is. Clothing stores that don't understand introversion have sales staff at the ready by the entrance, waiting for people to enter so they can approach them and immediately pose the dreaded question: "What can I do for you, sir?" Maybe this *is* polite, and friendly. But it's still not a good way to connect with us.

Give us some space, and let us look around first. Introverts need time to reflect on their own. We prefer to keep our trains of thought isolated from the influence of others. A simple "hello" when we enter the store is plenty.

Social finesse

Conversation topics can be a problem. Introverts often find casual small talk challenging.

"You have to try this sausage. It's from an amazing little farm near our summer house in Lyon."

Introverts often land hard in dialog, which can be a bit problematic: "No thanks, I just read an article about how sausages give you cancer."

Extraverts tend to be masters of the art of superficial, light, and balanced dialog. They can always find something to talk about with anybody, which is a great talent to have. They're really good at that simple, easy-going greeting: "Hey, how are you doing?" When an introvert asks that question, it doesn't mean "How are you doing?", but rather "How are you *really* doing?" We ask for the truth right from the get-go, because that's the only way we can see any value in asking. We listen intently to the response, even though we might be wearing our poker faces. This can make us come across as a little *too* intense at times, or a little too interested. We invest a lot of ourselves into these conversations, which can get a bit too heavy for an extraverted social butterfly. I've noticed that we tend to stay in conversations with people for a long time. I've been to several cocktail parties where I realized afterwards that I really only spoke to one person all evening. I'm nothing like a butterfly. I'm more like a vulture; I select my prey and dive after it. If my victim seems OK, i.e., isn't a blatant asshole, I refuse to let go. All or nothing! I've discussed this a lot with my introverted friends, and we seem to all have this strategy in common. The good thing about this approach to conversations is that on occasion, we'll come across somebody who feels *right*. Then, we'll suddenly find ourselves engaging in very deep and rewarding conversations with people whose names we didn't even know just five minutes earlier. It's as though we'd found a way to bypass all the layers of superficial courtesies, which allows us to speak openly about things that we feel strongly about. Introverts like to talk, make no mistake. But we want to make a deeper connection; we want conversations that go beyond the superficial level.

Can you detect introversion?

There are a number of different signs which are thought to reveal whether a particular person is an extravert or an introvert.

Here are some of the things that are said to be characteristic of extraverts:

- ✓ Answering questions immediately, without needing any time to think
- ✓ "Speaking with their hands", and lively facial expressions
- ✓ Touching the people they speak to
- ✓ Clothes, haircuts, and appearances that are intended to attract attention
- ✓ Bright colors, and lots of bling
- ✓ A conversational style that involves interrupting other people a lot

- ✓ Lots of eye contact
- ✓ Paying attention to everything that goes on around them, even things that aren't involved in the conversation

The following are characteristics of introverts:

- ✓ A Poker face
- ✓ A Monotonous tone of voice
- ✓ Laconic responses, preceded by pauses
- ✓ Thoughtfulness
- ✓ Maintaining a formal posture, and avoiding excessive physical contact with others
- ✓ Staring off into space when they think intensely
- ✓ Conservative clothing, with dull colors, usually grays, earthy colors, and black and white, giving them an unassuming appearance
- ✓ Repetitive clothing. For example, Facebook founder Mark Zuckerberg, has revealed that he owns twenty identical copies of the iconic gray T-shirt that his image has been formed around.
- ✓ Bowl cuts

There are thick books about how to *speed read* people in order to communicate better with them, convince them, deceive them, or attract them. In some cases, these books get it exactly right. I once spoke to a room full of introverted software developers. Everybody in the room really *was* wearing gray or black. However, we shouldn't disregard the fact that we live in a world in which we're all taught how to act in order to succeed in life. I know a girl who became a social outcast at work because of her colorful and expressive styling. This made her begin to dress much more modestly, and start tying her hair up in a bun. After this, she grew used to this more restrained style, and made it her own. If you were to try to determine her social preference based on the entries in the lists above, you'd probably place her in the wrong category.

Besides, we tend to act a little differently from one situation to the next. An old psychologist with an enormous beard once put it quite astutely: Who you are in a room depends on who else is in the room. If your colleagues are extremely introverted, it's easy for somebody less introverted to take on a more outgoing role. But when other people, who are more extraverted, join the group, it's also easy for that same person to shrink back and fall silent. While we do have a core personality, we're also shaped by the people and the environment around us. Sometimes we're more *active*, and other times we're more *reactive* —it's as simple as that. One of my friends is a well-disguised introvert. He spends a lot of time alone, working on different stuff. This means that he's fully charged when he meets people, and he tends to make a very alert and sociable impression. He jokes, pokes fun at himself, and talks with his hands. He wears ridiculously enormous scarves and stripy, loud sweaters, like some ad agency hipster. His appearance and behavior seem very extraverted to the casual observer, but he's actually an introvert.

In the early 2000s, a deluge of *how-to-get-laid* manuals was published. Neil Strauss' *The Game* is probably the most influential book in this genre. Here's a one-sentence summary of its message: the more you stand out from the crowd, the greater your chances are of receiving the affections you're craving.

Strauss discusses the *peacock effect*. He claims that being visually unique can help you in your quest for love, just like it helps the male peacock. The idea is that visual distinctiveness will signal the right kinds of things to the opposite sex. As a direct consequence of this idea, people are rocking some ridiculous looks in bars. Grown men are seriously wearing bright pink corduroy jackets, shirts with ruffles, and cowboy hats. Every other guy who's out for a night on the town is dressed like the CEO of some dot.com company during the heydays of the IT bubble. Visit any media business event, and you'll soon see what I mean.

Everybody's trying to look *special*, and I guess they do look special, but perhaps not in the way they intended. This is yet another example of how appearance, style, and personality don't always match up. Lots of quiet people have invented an extreme image for themselves as a way of forming connections with people like them. They often gather in some subculture or other. For example, the *goth* culture seems to suit introverts well. What might seem a little confusing is the fact that an introverted person chooses such an extreme style. In my experience, you generally can't tell what somebody's social preference is just by looking at them.

To determine whether somebody really is an introvert, you need to study their whole lifestyle. The classic signs won't match if the person in question has adapted to modern society. After all, we've all been taught that there's something wrong with being withdrawn and discrete. No, you need to know what people do when they're in their most natural state before you can draw any conclusions. One of the most talkative people I've ever met is a taxi driver. I asked him if he always enjoys meeting new people. He told me that he spends his weekends alone with his dog. They both go out to his cabin in the woods, and he doesn't talk to a soul. This is how he recharges his batteries. People who seem to be extremely outgoing might very well have a great need for alone time.

The innermost circle of hell is a mingling event

A few years ago, I would have preferred to jump naked on a huge pile of thumbtacks over going to a gala dinner. However, somewhere along the way, I've developed a better attitude about it.

My professional life places me in situations where I'm out of my natural element. I'm often required to be sociable with large numbers of people. Below, I'd like to give you some tips

I've collected over the years, which can make events of this kind enjoyable even for introverts.

A survival guide for mingling events

1. **The power of a word**. Legendary reporter Morley Safer said all it takes is one word: "Why?" A single word was all he needed to enter into a dialog with anybody. This word can transform small talk into a meaningful conversation. If somebody tells you that they've moved, or changed their job, or gone back to school, ask them: "Why?" Make sure to ask them in a way that expresses your curiosity and your friendly attitude. There's a difference between asking somebody a question and questioning somebody.
2. **Ride a party animal's coat tails**. If you have a friend who is a social genius, count yourself lucky! Follow her around, and use her as your ice breaker. With a person like that by your side, you can be as talkative as you choose.
3. **Catch your breath**. If you're feeling suffocated, go to the bathroom, stand on the balcony, or look at the decor. You don't need to explain where you're going. Why do people think they have to tell somebody where they're going all the time?
4. **The zombie stare**. Crowds used to make me uncomfortable. When I visited the Malmö Festival, I felt like a toad in a cattle stampede at times. A colleague of mine, who had learned to navigate the crowds of Calcutta, taught me a trick: don't look at anybody. As long as you don't look people in the eyes, they'll make room for you to pass. This works extremely well. Just wear your best dead eye stare and look right past everybody. This will make them think you can't see them, and cause them to get out of your way.

5. **Rapport**. Psychologist Milton Erickson noticed that his interactions with his patients were more effective when he discretely mimicked their body language. This technique makes it easier to achieve rapport. To use it, begin by observing how a person is standing, and how he or she sounds. If she speaks quickly and leans forward, you do the same. If she changes her posture, you do the same, but allow some time to pass first, so that it won't be too obvious. The theory here is that the smaller the contrast is between two people in terms of posture and voice, the easier it'll be for them to establish a relaxed mode of conversation.

6. **Listen**. The most obvious talent that introverts possess is the strongest play in the book in social situations. We're able to listen actively, without constantly looking for an opening for what we want to say. When a conversation becomes too demanding, you always have the choice of listening.

7. **The therapeutic angle**. Sigmund Freud noticed early on that his position during a session had great importance. He discovered that not sitting opposite his conversation partner had certain benefits. Eye contact seemed to disrupt the thought patterns of his clients. He preferred to sit diagonally across from the people he was speaking to. Freud has been described as extremely introverted, and this fact probably played some part in this. I can relate to this notion. I find sitting on a bench next to somebody that I'm conversing with relaxing, and that my batteries run out much quicker if we sit face to face.

8. **Conscious presence**. Taking classes that teach you to live in the present has become quite a trendy thing to do. This concept is called *mindfulness*. Introverts have a lot of noise going on inside their heads. Neurologically speaking, we're buzzing with internal activity. The concept of mindfulness can be used to great effect in our everyday lives. In an avalanche of

112

impressions, you choose to focus on a single thing. For instance, you could study people's shoes, or focus entirely on what your taste buds are telling you about the canapés. By choosing one thing to focus your attention on, you can find inner peace in even the worst case of Black Friday Frenzy.

Seating arrangements

Seating arrangements are the worst. The idea of sprinkling extraverts in among the reticent introverts, "to liven them up", is a foolproof way of causing people to experience anxiety. It's about as intelligent as peeing in the pool to make the water warmer. All it will usually give you is bored extraverts and clammed-up introverts. Many extraverts find the responsibility of keeping the conversation going to be quite a burden. The first faulty assumption here is that introverts need to be activated. Don't factor extraversion or introversion into your seating arrangements. Use shared interests as a guide instead.

Introverts often have a great time, even if they don't act out as much. Extraverts who are having fun do shots and dance on the table wearing necktie headbands. Introverts don't act like that when they get excited. We prefer to hang out by the bar sharing YouTube clips, and discussing why time is the fourth dimension.

Summary for extraverts

✓ If you want to communicate something important to an introvert, condense the message to three sentences or less.
✓ Introverts rarely express off-the-cuff opinions. We need time to think and reflect before we can make up our minds about things.
✓ Don't think that you can tell who's an introvert or an extravert just by looking at them. The only way to figure it out is to get to know the person well enough to know what they do to unwind.

Is introversion a disadvantage?

Have you ever considered how formidable leaders are portrayed on TV and in the movies? A recurring scene involves somebody needing to exchange a few words with the powerful leader. "Walk with me," the boss says, wrinkling his brow. They walk briskly through an open plan office. The boss is always a step or two ahead of the person who's seeking audience with him. He's too busy to slow down. During their conversation, the boss will also be delivering monologs to the people they pass by: "I need your report by three!", "Carl, sell twenty units and buy forty!", or "Great work, Karen! Keep it up and you'll have a great future at this company!" The idea that's being presented here is that a leader is somebody who thinks on the move, acts forcefully, and can communicate and think at the same time. This boss is somebody who knows that he wants, and has the ability to make immediate decisions. Basically, what we're looking at here is an extravert.

Unfortunately, this ideal doesn't match up with how introverted leaders handle their responsibilities.

I once worked in close collaboration with a young woman who was an extravert. We didn't understand each other very well. I realized that her definition of good teamwork was "I want to enter your office without making an appointment, twenty times an hour, to ask you stuff while you smile like an airline hostess and give me all the information I want, whenever I want it, and never ask me to write down any of the things you're telling me."

Sometimes, I had to concentrate, and closed my office door. Then, I'd see her making puppy eyes at me from the other side of the glass door. Once, when I had a lot on my mind, I emailed her a question instead of poking my head out of the door. She blew up at me. "It's insane that you're emailing me when we're sitting right next to each other!" If your communication style is introverted, you'll have to spend a lot of time defending it over the course of your professional life.

I hate being interrupted when I'm in the middle of something. This is because I'm completely immersed in my current activity. If somebody stops by to ask me something, it takes up my time in a way I can't plan for. The person who does this is never another introvert. All those polite phrases you need to say before you can ask a simple question take *time*. Even if answering the question doesn't take long, it'll take me some time to regain the focus I had before I was distracted. Introverts delve deep into things. Being interrupted is annoying. That's why I like to communicate by email. Email doesn't necessarily require the other person to interrupt what he or she is doing; they can simply read it when they have time. I think of it as a way of showing respect. Extreme extraverts tend to claim that it's much more efficient to just walk over and tap the person you need to ask something on the shoulder. "Check it out! That question got answered faster when we simply talked about it instead, didn't it?" This person is almost always the kind who likes to stick around for some small talk afterwards, which immediately cancels out any time that was saved by handling the issue verbally. The extravert will often forget to write down the answer, and therefore forget it completely. Half an hour later, the same person wanders back to you: "Hey, what did we decide before?" But the main problem is the one I mentioned earlier: *setup time*. One corporation investigated this phenomenon, and determined that each interruption, however brief, wasted an average of fifteen minutes of pure setup time.

Sometimes the introvert will never find her way back to what she was thinking about. It might be more efficient for extraverts to discuss things directly, face to face, but for introverts, email is often the better option. If it's difficult to put it in writing, just write this: "I need to talk to you. Call me, or come by when you have a moment." There's nothing wrong with the outgoing communication style per se, but it shouldn't automatically be given precedence either. Laying claim to somebody else's time is a way of exercising power. When you do this, you're showing them that your time is more valuable than theirs. This means that writing is a good approach in the right context.

But for me, it's mostly a matter of efficiency. Sometimes, interrupting somebody simply isn't the most efficient method. I require a certain degree of isolation to do focused and quality-oriented work. I often don't answer the phone, for this very reason. I don't act like this because of some dislike for the person who's calling me, it's just that the timing isn't good for me. I can always call them back later, when I'm not busy.

When introverts get to choose

A colleague of mine once put it quite vividly: "When I'm talking to really outgoing people, I feel like a hundred-year-old on a football field. Most of the time, the ball doesn't come my way, and I just stand there flat-footed, waiting. When I do somehow end up with the ball, I very rarely get anywhere near the end zone. Some fast dude always catches up with me and tackles me."

I recognize this feeling of never getting to finish a sentence. It becomes a source of stress, and I end up getting tongue-tied. Sometimes I'll stutter, or say something weird. If the extravert majority were to grant me one wish, I'd ask them to get better at waiting for the points that introverts try to get across to them. They're not all bad at this; there are plenty of extraverts who are amazing conversationalists, and have mastered the art of waiting. Similarly, some introverts could go on talking about their favorite topics until the person listening to them died of malnutrition.

The core issue here is the strong need to get to finish making your point.

I'd like to claim that this is why many introverts love social media, like Facebook and Twitter. Somebody said: "I'm an extravert online." This is an interesting way of putting it, which I support one hundred percent. Online, we get the time to phrase things properly, and finish our sentences. Correct spelling is another indication that the person you're dealing with is an introvert. Extraverts are the ones who answer party invitations by writing something and following it with fifteen exclamation marks. I also believe that the things we decide to share on social media are greatly determined by our social preferences. The extremely outgoing people are usually the ones who find value in taking pictures of the foam on their lattes, or writing about how much they're enjoying their gourmet coffee with soy milk. Extraverts show close-ups of their most insignificant moments, to make themselves stand out from all the digital noise. To an introvert, that noise just seems superficial. Introverts often write a different kind of posts on social media sites.

Take a look at your own friend list, and see if you agree: extraverts write posts and status updates that are mainly about themselves. They post a lot of pics of "me holding my drink and smiling in front of the sunset." Introverts tend to write posts in which they take a stand on some issue or other, or spread some particular piece of information. We share links, or write about things that matter deeply to us.

One of the consequences of the current media culture is that the number of people in your friends list will often determine the value of your opinions. Many online contests are judged according to the principle of "whoever gets the most likes is the winner." Therefore, the participants will often ask their friends to "go there and like my contribution, so I can win this contest!" This means that it's no longer about your performance, or your credentials; what matters is simply how many people you know.

118

One look says it all

Back when I was a teenager, the parents of one of my friends decided that they didn't trust me. They based this on the fact that I didn't make eye contact with them to the extent that they felt a trustworthy person should. In the West, there's a fairly widespread idea that trustworthiness is expressed through distinct attributes such as *a good firm handshake* or *a steady gaze*. We can learn all of these behaviors, of course, but we should bear in mind that the particular things that signal trust are all culturally determined.

I was once in a meeting with a group of consultants from India. They were polite and friendly in every way, but I did notice that they all stared at the table during most of our meeting. There's nothing strange about this behavior at all. India is a country with other ideals than the ones we have in the West. There, looking somebody in the eyes is a way of challenging them. The same is true of many animals. You might investigate how a Rottweiler reacts if you make eye contact with it, just as long as you make sure it's on a leash first.

Then, something strange happened to those guys from India. Their employer arranged for them to take a class on Swedish culture. The next time I saw them, they stared deeply into my eyes throughout the conversation. Their foreheads were pretty sweaty, probably because of how uncomfortable this made them. Unfortunately, nobody had explained the 30/70 rule to them, i.e., the idea that the right amount of eye contact is about 70 percent of the conversation.

At this point, it's worth adding that taking unsteady eyes to signify a lack of interest is a classic mistake. As I've mentioned, introverts will often look away in order to focus better on what's happening inside their minds. It helps us visualize the things we're being told.

The dark side...

The expression *going postal* was phrased during the 1980s, when a number of shootings occurred in quick succession at US post offices. The perpetrators were all loyal employees, and most of them had seemed quiet and unassuming until they suddenly exploded with rage.

If we disregard mass shootings for a moment, many people consider suddenly erupting in anger to be a trait of introverts. This may seem a little strange, considering that the stereotypical image of an introvert is somebody who's about as temperamental as Steven Wright or Droopy. I'd like to puncture this myth. Their calm is a facade, which covers up the anger, happiness and love they experience beneath it, every bit as intensely as an extravert would. There's a dynamic aspect to emotions that's worth knowing about. Extraverts are quick to act on their emotions. They project their feelings onto their surroundings, which means that you can usually tell what kind of day an extravert is having quite easily. They vent their emotions constantly. Introverts tend to gather negative emotions inside themselves, in a huge pressure cooker full of feelings. The emotions that fill us up take a long time to abate. This means that we're often sensitive to impressions. If I hear a song with sad lyrics, I'll see nothing but gray skies all afternoon. Some films have had a strong effect on me, and weighed on my thoughts for days after I saw them. Rage affects us in a similar way. Unfortunately, this has made resentfulness a characteristic of introverts. We often bite our tongues when something annoys us, rather than telling people about it. At most, we might write an angry letter to the newspaper, or post an angry note to our neighbors in the stairwell. But we can also channel our rage into valuable activities. Sometimes, we use it for constructive ends. Many a den and wooden deck has been created this way. Sometimes, our hobbies aren't enough, and our emotions get the better of us. The dams of stability break, and surprised onlookers witness us becoming mad as holy hell. A long time can pass between introverts' eruptions, sometimes even decades. If you have extraverted children, you're bound to lose your temper several times a day, irrespective of your own social preference.

Studies have shown that the temperaments of introverts and extraverts are different. Extraverts are more in touch with *positive* emotions. They smile, giggle, laugh, cry tears of joy, and shriek with glee. They rest on a solid foundation of positive thoughts, which affects their outlook on life. I've become convinced that the world of a true extravert is just like a musical.

Introverts are far more likely to focus on the negative aspects of their emotions. We're more cynical, pessimistic, and disillusioned, basically. More like Tim Burton, and less like Mel Brooks. One advantage here is that, to some extent, pessimism makes you more thick-skinned. As an introvert, you're likely to be your own worst critic. This means that few of the things that others criticize you for will come as surprises. After all, you already know about your own flaws and weaknesses. You've already thought of every possible criticism yourself. This lends you some stability. Falling over doesn't hurt when you're already lying down.

Prejudice

I'm riding the train with the other commuter zombies on a dreary Tuesday. I have a pounding headache after giving an intense lecture. I feel like somebody's watching me. I look up, and see a guy who looks a bit like a gangster, staring at me. He's tall, and has a powerful build and a crew cut. He's wearing a worn leather jacket which is at least a decade old. He stares right at me, without even trying to hide it. I avoid his gaze by pretending to send text messages. He scans me from top to bottom, without so much as a hint of embarrassment. My pulse rises, and my headache makes me extra irritable. There's conflict in the air. I take a deep breath and stare back at him. I choose not to shift my gaze at all, like a real caveman. Our staring contest last for what seems like an eternity, but is really only a few seconds, until he suddenly says, in a Halland accent: "That's a nice color for you to wear, you look good in pink." He smiles.

This wasn't irony, sarcasm, or a junkie's ramblings. It was something much worse: pure, unadulterated friendliness.

I was ashamed that I'd been so quick to judge this situation a threat. My interpretation was based on prejudice. If it had been an elderly lady in a loden coat who was staring at me, I would never have interpreted things the way I did.

Studies have shown that extraverts and introverts interpret encounters with strangers differently. Generally speaking, introverts are more pessimistic, and more suspicious of strangers. I'd like to claim that this is because we have a better understanding of things. It actually *is* a bad idea to buy a wristwatch from one of the vendors on the beach in Tijuana. An extravert will tend to see a potential future friend where an introvert sees Hannibal Lector. Introverts are generally suspicious of strangers. The stranger I met on that train was right though, I *do* look pretty good in pink. Suspicion is a heavy suit of armor to wear, and it can be more cumbersome than protective in certain situations.

Unfortunately, associating mass murderers with intro-version seems to be a popular trend in the media these days. They often seem to fit the mold of a "young man who's isolated himself from social interaction, and lost his sense of empathy." The terrible massacre on Utøya island was committed by a man who was described as isolated and introverted, but who proved to have much more to his story than that. In court, he maintained eye contact throughout his questioning, and seemed untroubled by the massive attention he was getting. Anders Behring Breivik is probably something else. I don't know what he is, but he's no introvert.

In Denver, a man walked into an opening night screening of the new Batman movie. Some people noticed his striking, bright orange hair. Suddenly, he produced his firearms, and fired into the panicking crowd at random. In his own mind, he was one of the characters in the movie. Since this event occurred, people who knew him have described him as an exceptionally bright and introverted student. As I'm writing this, a twenty-four-year-old man has just shot eighteen children at a school in the USA. We're seeing the exact same pattern from Denver repeat itself: mass murderer Adam Lanza is also being described as an introverted genius.

The core issue with people like these isn't whether they're introverts or extraverts. These people have serious personality disorders, and their issues really go far beyond that particular dichotomy. The histories of serial and mass murder offer examples of both extraverts and introverts. Smooth-talker Glen Rogers traveled across the USA, killing people along the way after winning them over with his charm. Ted Bundy, perhaps the most notorious serial killer of all, who killed thirty women before he was apprehended, has been described as an extraverted person.

So, the idea that there's some over-representation of introversion among these people is basically a myth.

Do extraverts have an easier time?

Here's a letter I received within a week of this book's publication date. Since then, I've received variations of this letter many times, from people of all ages. The letter is less concerned with the writing in my book, and more concerned with the word I chose to use as its title.

Hi Linus!

My name is Maria. I've read your book, and I have to say that it changed my life, as well as how I think of myself. It opened up a whole new world to me, and I've read up on the subject even more since then. I can't understand how I've been so ignorant of this my whole life. I've always thought that there was something wrong with me, and that I needed to change. Now, I've realized that I'm an introvert, and I've begun to accept and embrace my characteristics instead. I don't feel like the odd one out any more. I've found a completely new appreciation for myself, and for the first time in my life, I'm content with who I am.

Thanks Linus, for drawing attention to this incredibly important topic!

But do extraverts have an easier time?

Extraverts are energized by conversations, and Introverts are energized by silence. If there's one things missing in the world today, it's silence.

The WHO treats introversion as a *mental disorder*. Some of us find that a little offensive. It's kind of like referring to redheads as pigmentally challenged. It's worth remembering that the very same organization claimed that homosexuality was a disease until 1990. I find it strange that somebody would think that introversion was some kind of disability. Research on this has shown beyond any doubt that this preference has its advantages. Introverts tend to excel at things like academic achievement, impulse control, visualization, independent thinking, and structure.

When I was growing up, it was brought home to me on a number of occasions that being an introvert wasn't always considered OK. I remember one occasion, when we went on a skiing trip with my cousins. We weren't allowed to spend any time in the cabin during the daytime. Oh no, we had to spend as much time as possible outdoors, getting good value out of our ski lift tickets. I remember how empty I felt inside when I had all of these impressions forced upon me. As soon as I was allowed to go back to the cabin, I escaped into my comic books and isolated myself, to recharge. Travel has never appealed to me much. There's plenty for me to see inside my own mind. When we made a road trip through England, my eyes were glued to my newest, biggest love: a book about astronomy. This annoyed everybody else. I could tell they were frustrated by everything they felt I was missing.

My parents looked at mangy old sheep, closed-down factories, and the perpetual English rain, but I was learning about the whole universe! It's far from a given who was really having the most interesting time. But it's also strange that things should be this way. After all, nobody would ever accuse an extravert of *paying too much attention* during a holiday.

It's easy to get jealous of an extravert who travels to some health resort, and then proceeds to get to know every single person within a three-mile radius. The pool guy, the bartender, the receptionist, even the gardener's color-blind half-brother; he makes friends with everybody. There's a particular kind of extravert, who can really brighten up a whole room with their charisma. They effortlessly find their ways into any conversation, and can joke and play around with their friends for hours, remaining spontaneous and expressive the whole time. They enjoy restaurants the best when they're full of people. They love the hustle and bustle of a busy market square. Extraversion is a gift, but so is introversion. Everything I've mentioned has a cost, and we pay it in the only currency we really have: time. Calling another person up on the phone is an investment. If you decide to spend the same amount of time writing a page of your book instead, that's an investment too.

I need to invest my time in my writing. I enjoy closing the door to my office, and sitting down in my comfortable armchair. Black coffee and the right tunes are all the company I need on an ordinary day. I can work away for hours on end. Sometimes, I've seen whole nights go by this way. I've been so comfortably enfolded in my own thoughts that I've completely lost track of time, and attained a powerful state of flow. My introversion becomes a cocoon constructed from my own imaginary worlds. This experience is simultaneously harmonious and intense,

To answer the question of whether extraverts have an easier time, here are my own thoughts on the matter:

It's easier to *fit in* with society if you're an extravert.

However, it's easier for an introvert to find contentedness.

We don't need to be activated, and we're very seldom bored. For us, having to wait for something simply means that we get some time to relax. To us, solitude is a word that has more positive connotations than negative ones.

Summary for extraverts

✓ It's easy for an introverted person to feel content. They don't need much in the way of variety or social interaction. In this respect, introversion simply means being self-sufficient in terms of energy.
✓ Introverted people are often more comfortable with communicating in writing. It gives them time to reflect, and shields them from interruption.
✓ Telephones strike fear in introverts. We generally avoid making phone calls unless we have something very specific to discuss.

Solitude vs. Loneliness

Blam!

The shot went off in my hands. I could feel the winter cold radiate through my body. All I could hear was the wind whistling around the bombed-out concrete structure. My captain glared at me. "Bad call Jonkman, bad f***ing call." Somehow, my combat belt had gotten caught in the gun I was carrying. The bullet I'd fired was only a blank, but the symbolic implications were very serious. My captain was hard as flint, and had lost one of his thumbs in an accidental shooting. He punished me by withholding my privileges. I was confined to the barracks for a whole month. I couldn't take part in activities like the town festival and the bar nights, and I wasn't allowed to join the other guys in my platoon for the Thursday night dances, and all the other stuff they did. They felt bad for me. One guy lent me his CD player so that I could listen to music while I sat there alone at night. They smuggled beers in for me, to boost my morale. Somebody brought me some video tapes to watch. That month was really rough on me... or at least, it was in *their* minds. If you ask me, that time was one of the highlights of my military service. Instead of being constantly surrounded by people, I got to spend long evenings alone with my sketch pad, listening to soul music. I loved it. I played along, and acted as though I felt that the punishment was severe, because that's what everybody else seemed to think. After all, we all want to be normal, whatever that means.

Introverts can live in confined spaces, in humble conditions, and still be content, as long as they get to be alone now and then My daughter's godfather claims that all he needs to be satisfied with life is sufficient space for his desk, his laptop, and his camera.

The perks of solitude

The word *loneliness* certainly has negative connotations for most people. It implies involuntary social isolation, which is a depressing notion. There's something sad about lonely people who don't have anybody to share their lives with. But then there's another word: *solitude*. This word describes a state of voluntary isolation, which is tranquil and harmonious instead. A wise Buddhist once pointed out that loneliness isn't a matter of whether or not there are any other people around. You can feel lonely even in the company of others. And you can feel connected to people who live on the other side of the world. Whether or not you're lonely doesn't have anything to do with how many words you utter, or how loud your voice is. Somebody who speaks to every single person at the market square could still be the loneliest person in the world. I'm convinced that many of our biggest celebrities feel quite lonely. Like Byron said: "a celebrity is one who is known to many persons he is glad he doesn't know." Lonely is what you are if you don't have any love in your life. Being *alone* doesn't necessarily mean that you're *lonely*.

One of the great gifts of introversion is the ability to enjoy your own company. Einstein said that he'd found being alone painful as a young man, but enjoyable once he'd reached a more mature age. Punishing an introvert with solitude is like trying to drown a fish.

Introvert Carina describes a memorable moment of solitude:

> *It happened one day towards the end of summer, in my own back of the woods in Dalarna, a province in the middle of Sweden. I had walked for several miles, hiking right up the mountainside, when the forest suddenly opened up. An enormous fen spread out before me. There were so many cloudberries growing there that the ground was speckled with bright amber*

dots as far as I could see. I walked in silence, alone, enjoying the stillness, the scents, and the distant rustle of the treetops. I sat down to rest on a high tree trunk. Suddenly, I heard a humming noise behind me. I turned around, and saw a small whirlwind moving to and fro. It was skipping over tufts of grass and brush, making its way towards me in a slithering, winding fashion. I followed it with my eyes, and felt a strange sense of calm come over me. It stopped in front of my feet, where it did its playful dance for a while, before continuing away across the fen. Then and there, it was just nature and myself, a tiny moment that was absolutely enormous.

Being in nature, on my own, or with somebody who's able to spend time with me in silence, is one of my favorite things to do. In silence, in stillness, or by a raging sea, I can replenish my energy and my strength. Sometimes, when life get messy and noisy, I take refuge in my thoughts, and return to my tree trunk by the fen to re-experience that stillness.

You're truly lonely if you can't enjoy being alone

The way I see it, needing other people around all the time is a weakness.

Evidently, being an introvert is no obstacle to finding a spot in the limelight. The King of Pop, Michael Jackson, must be the strongest proof of this. He was a very withdrawn person, who suffered from Peter Pan syndrome, and spent most of his time alone in a castle. It's surprising how often introverted stars adopt a macabre stage persona. It's as though they were rebelling against their own private personalities. Marilyn Manson's extreme outfits and image are far removed from the shy person he becomes once the stage lights go out. David Bowie flirted with different identities as well, inventing colorful alter egos like Ziggy

Stardust. He described these personas as a way for him to overcome his stage fright. In interviews, he stated that he'd felt like an alien for most of his life. The fact that Bob Dylan very rarely gives interviews has been the object of some discussion in the media. Some people have chosen to interpret it as the hubris of an aged rock god. But anybody who has truly studied and followed Bob's career will see a different pattern emerge: he's not arrogant, he's an introvert.

Generally speaking, extraverts are assumed to dominate the world of pop music, while introverts are supposedly more numerous within the world of classical music. And in the world of comedy, introversion is often regarded as a professional characteristic of stand-up comedians. Jerry Seinfeld's oddball and introverted style has won him fame across the globe. He constructs his performances in solitude, meticulously combining humorous observations from everyday life into a set of jokes that he delivers to the masses. It makes total sense. Comedy is largely based on observations of things that other people do. Introverts are observers, and comedian Larry David exemplifies this role better than anybody else.

Introversion is thought to be the dominant trait in the world of fine art. Picasso even said that "without great solitude, no serious work is possible."

I'd like to *want* to be more sociable. But I'm also quite comfortable with being uncomfortable in groups. I've accepted that this is simply how I feel. I do like people, but I don't feel the urge to be near them all the time, and that doesn't make me any less happy. A study was performed to investigate what happens when introverts pretend that they're extraverts, and act accordingly. The introverted test subjects were instructed to smile a lot, speak a lot, and initiate contact with strangers. After a while, the test subjects reported that acting as though they were happy had actually made them happier. However, this experiment was based on the assumption that happiness is the same thing to all people. But we differ from one another in this respect. Something that makes an extravert happy won't necessarily do the job for an introvert. Extraverts' happiness is all energy and excitement. It lifts people's spirits, and makes them order whole bottles of tequila and shriek with joy. It's all about umbrella drinks, spontaneous dancing, and lots of high-fiving. The countless talent shows on TV present great examples of extraverted characteristics. The participants weep for joy, and jump and skip frantically whenever somebody gives them even the smallest of compliments. When they win, they scream in a tone of voice that's only audible to dogs. I could never do that. Putting me on a show like that would be a disaster. The idea of me as a contestant on "*Idol*" is more fantastic than anything that happens in the *Star Wars* trilogy.

Introverts' happiness expresses itself differently. It's a feeling of contentedness and harmony, that doesn't involve any yelling or jumping. The fact that we're prepared to settle for that can make us seem miserable to extraverts: "Poor you, sitting here alone all night." I think it must be very impractical to have to go to all that trouble to feel any satisfaction.

My happiest moments tend to come after darkness has fallen. My kids, tired after daycare, sit down on my lap with their bottles. We sit on the couch together, watching *Finding Nemo* for the 300th time. We snuggle until they fall asleep. I hold a small hand in mine, and rest my chin on my son's head. That's all I need to feel at home, both literally and figuratively. It's not about laughter and fireworks, it's a deep and warm sense of belonging, and gratitude. I'd choose that over waving glow sticks around at a rave any day.

Summary for extraverts

✓ Introverts' need for solitude and integrity can be mistaken for arrogance and disapproval.
✓ Introverts have an easy time experiencing happiness and joy, but we often show it in a more restrained way than extraverts do.
✓ Introverts are seldom lonely. We enjoy our own company, and don't mind going without intense communication with others for extended periods of time.

How Introverts and Extraverts Relate to Each Other

"I'm sorry." The doctor, whose name was full of consonants, looked at us. His Swedish was pretty broken, but what he was saying was impossible to misunderstand. Despite his professional calling, this was difficult for him. I thought that delivering this kind of news was something that became routine after a while, but that didn't seem to be the case. Two words closed the door to our future. It was a strange feeling. I backed up into myself, as though I was wrapping myself around the pain, to encapsulate it inside myself.

We hugged each other for a long time, without speaking. It got dark outside. Hanna fell asleep. I tucked her in, and sat down on the edge of the bed. From that point, we took different paths, even though we were living in the same space. We'd lost the child we'd been expecting. Something had gone wrong in the biological game of chance. Nobody could say why. Hanna chose to open up, and speak to the people she was close to about it. She vented her feelings, and shared her burden with anybody who had room to spare in their hearts. I had no words at all, just a huge load of thoughts. I swallowed these thoughts down as deep as I could, and then I brooded. They were always there in the back of my mind, filling my existence. The world around me saw a Linus who hadn't let it get to him. I became manic, and took on everything my work could throw at me with great energy and focus. Over the next few years, we went through several miscarriages. One day, my happiness would be through the roof, and the next day I'd be stuck in a bottomless pit. It was an emotional rollercoaster unlike anything I'd ever experienced before. Sometimes, grief can strengthen a relationship, but in our case, it tore us apart, because of how differently we handled it. I carried mine on the inside, while Hanna shared hers with her friends. She was emotional. Her moods shifted back and forth in brief cycles. As for me, I went cold. I convinced myself that I had to maintain my stability. I imagined that I was some kind of anchor for her.

One of the differences between extraverted and introverted personalities lies in how they relate to emotions. Extraverts are often good at expressing positive emotions. Hanna was just as happy every time she found out she was pregnant. After the first miscarriage, I became skeptical. The next time the pregnancy test showed two lines, I chose to believe that it wouldn't work out. This way, I could ensure that I wouldn't be disappointed. My pessimism became a source of security. Call it an innate strategy – introverts use it for pretty much everything. Psychologists call this neuroticism. It's characterized by pessimism and a skeptical attitude to the events that unfold around us: every silver lining has a cloud, as I always say. Unfortunately, this also means that introverts are suspicious of strangers. Global studies have shown that because of this, in the Western world, extraverts are happier than introverts. They're probably more gullible as well, because they buy into the things they're told by smarmy sales guys. I don't know how many times I've saved Hanna from getting involved in pyramid selling schemes.

After five miscarriages, we'd lost all hope. Then, we were referred to a doctor who specialized in cases like ours. He included us in his study, and Hanna was excited. I was apathetic. He gave her a drug that had worked for other couples. When Hanna got pregnant again, she was overjoyed. I was apathetic. The weeks passed, and then Hanna suddenly began bleeding. This was a sign we'd already learned all about. It meant there was no hope. She was devastated. I was apathetic. We went in for a checkup, a procedure we were very familiar with by this point. I was watching a blurred TV while the ultrasound drew static on the screen. Hanna couldn't quite get herself to look at the screen. To my great surprise, I suddenly saw something on the screen: a small, pulsating dot. "There's the heart!" I blurted out. In that moment, all of my emotions were awakened at once. Everything came to the surface. Tears poured out of me. That throbbing little dot grew into the most amazing little girl you could imagine.

I think there's something in this story that anybody who's in an introvert/extravert relationship can relate to. Everybody goes through sorrow at some point in their life. Understanding what happens to us in those situations can be the thing that keeps the relationship going. It's been said that stress makes us *more* of whatever we are. An extravert will become more outgoing, more eager to connect with others, and more impulsive than before, while an introvert will become more withdrawn, more reflective, and more distanced.

Strangely enough, once we've been under stress for long enough, we enter into a truly destructive phase in which we become our own opposites. When an extravert falls silent, and begins to keep his door closed, you might be wise to tread carefully. When an introvert decides to act like an outgoing and dominant networking ace, it can be a sign of exhaustion. Others tend to notice how out of place this behavior seems, and pick up on the mixed signals that they're being given. We can often sense that something's wrong when we meet people who are in this phase.

In retrospect, I can safely say that I was neither feeling nor acting like myself during this time. I don't think I've ever taken on such an outgoing role at work as I did then. I was aggressive and energetic. I was probably a real jerk, too. I wasn't in a very good place.

Introverts have a tendency to keep their sadness inside. Then, we digest it until it's been dissolved completely by solitude and brooding. This is called internalizing; it's how we learn to relate to the things that trouble us.

Emotional leakage

Not all extraverts act like Miss Piggy. Reactive and outgoing people can often seem unstable to introverts. Their shifting moods can cause us to back away from them, and make us feel insecure in their company. I'd like to point out once more that introverts are just as prone to mood swings as extraverts. The difference simply lies in how we act out our emotions. Introverts are more sensitive to stimuli, which can make us interpret people's behavior as more significant than it actually is. We're very perceptive of subtle tones and hints. When an extravert raises her voice, she might not mean much by it: "My blood sugar was just a little low, sorry!" But the effects of her outburst can stay with the introvert for a long time. We can't stop trying to figure out what it was all about, and we think a lot about the consequences. This brooding usually continues long after the extravert has forgotten the whole thing ever happened.

One of my more extraverted acquaintances has confessed to occasionally feeling the urge to cause conflicts. She gets bored without some drama in her life. When she's with a quiet partner, she has to produce this excitement herself. She's described how she's sometimes pretended to take offense over some minor statement her boyfriend made. She's single now.

I have a truly extraverted colleague, who has a knack for always voicing controversial opinions in discussions. He can say things like "dictatorship is a great political system," or bring up abortion, and then proceed to disagree with whatever the other person thinks about the issue. He does this to cause tension, drama, and powerful emotions. He loves that stuff. Openly emotional people make me very uncomfortable; it's not something I'm used to. I'm especially terrified by people who can shift from happiness to raging anger in a matter of seconds. They make me think of that psychopathic woman who boiled a rabbit in *Fatal Attraction*.

No man is an island. Everybody has some need of

company, and to feel that they belong. It's a basic aspect of the human condition. What sets us apart from one another is how strongly we feel this need. Extraverts need company as an *activity*. Other people are like a hobby to an extravert, because that's where they get their energy from. When extraverts spend time together, it's like an energy potluck.

One small step for man, and one giant leap for geekdom

I don't think of the word *geek* as a derogatory term. To me, it simply denotes a person who pursues an interest with great passion, and is rather unapologetic about it. A true geek doesn't worry about whether or not collecting Smurfs is trendy. I know this, because I've been a geek my whole life. When I was a child, I was an avid birdwatcher. I cycled around on my own, with a pair of binoculars around my neck, and imagined that I was seeing lots of exotic birds everywhere I went. For my ninth birthday, I asked for a stuffed pheasant. My classmates wanted Meccano kits, He-Man's Castle Grayskull, or Star Wars TIE fighters. But I just sat there in my braces, with my dusty old bird, feeling on top of the world.

In my teens, I moved on to playing a lot of role-playing games. If I were to admit to how many hours of my life I've spent playing video games, it would make a lot of people concerned. It's never mattered to me what other people think, or how popular something is. This has occasionally kept me from being accepted into the popular circles, but I've never concerned myself with that; I've been too busy doing things that interested me. Nothing will make you lonelier than being dependent on the approval of others. In this sense, a geek is an independent soul.

Neil Armstrong, who was a legendary geek and a true hero, passed on in 2012. Despite his introverted nature, he conquered the most unexplored place of all, and set foot on the moon. I mentioned introverts' tendency to be cautious, prone to suffering stress, and risk-aware. Why would a person like that climb on top of 400 feet of explosives and shoot himself into space? I think I understand the dual aspects of Mr. Armstrong's choice, and I don't think he was afraid. Because of his geekiness, the curiosity and passion he experienced were probably strong enough to overshadow any fear he might have felt. His personality remained low-key even after he returned from the moon. He always used to say that "all I did was my job." I think that the meticulous attention to detail and the extremely detailed procedures that are required in preparing for and carrying out a journey into space seem perfectly suited for an introverted personality. We're passionate about details, and we can get very invested in discussions about which web browser is the best, or why Jean-Luc Picard is the best captain the Enterprise ever had. An introverted consultant I worked with had an incredible sense of detail. One day, he very carefully went over a bunch of accounts for a big corporation. All of a sudden, he found almost four million dollars in an account that everybody else had missed. Details are important, and as a mathematician once said: "I'd rather get something completely wrong than almost right."

The thing about stress

Suddenly, there's a loud noise in the bathroom. Hanna reacts quickly, and is on her feet before I've even moved. She yanks the door open, and sees that one of the water hoses has come loose from the bathroom wall. It's swaying around like an angry cobra, spraying hot water everywhere. I'm still in the armchair, observing what's happening. Hanna rushes into the bathroom, and grabs a little mat from the floor. Then, she stands there, paralyzed, clutching the mat to herself. This seems to be the full extent of her plan to save the day. "Come on! Do something!" she screams at me. But I'm doing plenty; I'm thinking and analyzing. It occurs to me that the mains tap is in the next room, so I dash over there to turn the water off.

These are both typical examples of how people with the different social preferences react to stress. Stress activates extraverts. They seize the initiative right away, and take action. Introverts shut down instead. We get overstimulated, and become passive and withdrawn. As long as the stress levels aren't too extreme, though, there are some positives to this. Our introverted calm allows us to think things through, rather than just react. We maintain a level of awareness that allows us to solve the problem. The US army has studied people's reactions to the stress of combat. They determined that extraverts were quick to react in scenarios that they'd been trained for in advance. If you throw a hand grenade into the trench they're in, they'll do what they've been taught to do, with incredible speed. Extraverts reacted quickly, and correctly. Introverts, on the other hand, performed well in unexpected situations, which they hadn't received any training for. To put it briefly: introverts *reflect*, and extraverts *react*.

One of things Neil Armstrong was famous for was how well he kept his cool in emergencies. This gift served him well during his years as a test pilot. I've thought about this in more general terms. I've seen people close to me go through difficult times in their lives, such as divorces, goodbyes, chronic diseases, financial difficulties, and other unpleasant stuff. Extraverts tend to act out their problems. They regress into attention-craving teenagers. They'll suddenly begin working out, get a tattoo, buy an acoustic guitar, or get a new trendy haircut. They'll often buy themselves a more youthful wardrobe. Sometimes, they turn into social vampires, and cling to others in order to leech energy from them. Introverts turn inward instead. We isolate ourselves playing *Counterstrike*, reading long novels, or embroidering horses on stuff. We stay awake until the

141

small hours of dawn, reading stuff on the Internet and half-watching "Bionic Mutant Teenagers from Outer Space" on the TV. Suddenly, after a few days, weeks, or months, we're done. Somehow, we've broken down all that negative stuff inside, and hauled it away; we're ready to move on. Introverts have an undeniable need for time to reflect. In relationships with extraverts, it can be difficult for us to get them to accept this behavior. Wanting to spend time alone can make you seem reclusive or selfish.

In our society, an introvert's mourning process is considered unhealthy, while the extravert way of handling grief is regarded as completely normal. Comforting yourself with a serious bender, and going through the whole throwing up, crying, and getting into fights cycle is just something that people do. Even waking up on strangers' couches five days a week can be thought of as healthy: "Let her get it out of her system, she's going through a rough patch." Extraverts and introverts may go through different processes, but neither of them is inherently more appropriate than the other.

Self-discipline

In the 1970s, a psychologist named Walter Mischel put a bunch of children into a series of closed rooms. He was performing an experiment for the Stanford University, and the results he arrived at would end up making him famous.

Each child received a marshmallow, and was told that if they could wait a few minutes before eating the marshmallow, they would be given another one. Each time they were able to refrain from eating their marshmallows, they received another. It was soon apparent that these children possessed very different levels of self-discipline. Some of them immediately devoured their marshmallows, while others would wait for several cycles, and end up with piles of goodies in front of them. The psychologist realized that there were two different attitudes at play here. One of the groups was very focused on the present; on the things they could see and feel in the here and now. This was the group that couldn't wait, because they wanted immediate rewards. The other group was more future-oriented, and looked forward to later rewards. The truly interesting thing is that these children were tested again as adults. The children who had stronger willpower back in the 1970s were more often successful in life as adults, and scored higher on standardized tests than those who were less disciplined.

This is interesting, because introverts tend to have better impulse control than extraverts do. Extraverts are very invested in the here and now. That's why they pay more attention to, and are more susceptible to, the influence of the particular stimuli that their senses register in the moment. The strengths of introverts are afterthought and analysis, and the ability to postpone rewards. This has been corroborated by MRI studies in which the differences between the brains of extraverts and introverts have been identified. It's hard to give a definition of the concept of willpower, because it has so many different meanings and aspects.

Extraverts can perform amazingly well in competitions. It's as though the very excitement of competing boosts their abilities. If somebody proudly announces that they're an alpha, you can pretty much tell which side of the spectrum they're on just from that. An introvert is more likely to be a delta, i.e., somebody who doesn't bother comparing themselves to others in terms of status at all.

On the other hand, the willpower of introverts has to do with being able to stay focused on a single thing for an extended period of time. We dig into a task, and don't ease off until it's finished. The willpower of extraverts expresses itself differently. They have a great capacity for getting things done by social means. Presenting a united front this way can be a very powerful thing. A psychologist once said something that I agree with: introverts have great *willpower*, while extraverts have great *changing power*.

One thing at a time

Introversion has far-reaching implications for our awareness of the present. We carry a bubble around with us wherever we go. I've often had reason to reflect on how amazing extraverts are at being in the present. Their senses are very strongly rooted in what's happening in the here and now. They keep tabs on everyone in the room, and notice it whenever anybody leaves or enters it. If you're in a discussion with an extravert in a café, your conversation partner will be able to keep track of what's going on at three other tables while you're both talking, without getting distracted.

This is a great knack to have for people who have small children. My extraverted younger brother Anton doesn't miss anything that happens in his presence. His parental radar allows him to evade incoming marmalade sandwiches and catch falling milk cartons inches before they hit the ground, all while praising his daughter's drawings, enthusiastically discussing skater fashion, and doing something or other on his iPhone. This is characteristic of the *multitasking* extraverted personality.

Being an introvert, I find doing more than one thing at a time to be quite challenging. This isn't something I've chosen, it's a consequence of the biological hardware I was born with. I can listen to music while I work, as long as it's a tune I know by heart. But the moment I try to do something else at the same time, my brain capacity is out the window. An example of this is what sometimes happens when I'm on the phone. If the other party is too talkative, my mind will often wander. While I'm half-listening to them, I'll often look something or other up on the computer. "Linus, that's your computer voice again." People who know me always catch me out. Many hairdressers are extraverts, which explains how they're able to keep a conversation going while they cut people's hair. If I tried to do something like that, I'd end up with a lawsuit on my hands.

A boss I had once told me in a performance review that he felt I should practice *multitasking*. I understand now that what he was expressing was an extraverted norm. I've learned that it's not a good working method for introverts, and I'll admit that I was pleased to read the recent studies that show that *multitasking* has an adverse effect on quality and adds setup time to tasks, which basically means that it's inefficient. The most efficient way to work is to finish one task before moving on to the next.

Our sequential thinking is one of the reasons why some psychologists claim that introversion is actually a mild form of autism, and similarly, that ADHD is an extension of extraversion.

Dominance

Psychologists have studied how we choose our relationships. In brief, it tends to go like this: we choose friends who are like ourselves, but romantic partners who aren't. Introverts, especially, tend to be attracted to extraverts. We seem to seek similarity in our friends, but differences in the people we choose to spend our lives with. We're attracted to the qualities that we don't have. The trite old compliment "you complete me" actually makes pretty good sense.

In an introvert/extravert relationship, the latter tends to be the dominant party. Dominance is often thought to be a purely negative thing, but I'd like to challenge that notion. Introverts will enter a reflective state of mind when faced with a decision. We turn the issue every which way in our minds, and we're quite prone to over-analyzing things. We see all the grays, instead of just black and white.

Extraverts approach things more directly. When I was asked to write this book, I spent the whole day deliberating on whether or not to accept the offer. I weighed the impact it would have on my busy schedule, and considered how my free time, my finances, and everything else I could think of would be affected. It felt like a difficult decision, so I emailed Hanna at work. She responded within a minute: "Of course you should write it! Say yes!!!" This was her whole analysis of the offer. As I pointed out earlier, *only* extraverts use that many exclamation marks.

Hanna's response shows how quickly extraverts make up their minds. They make speedy decisions, often basing them on their initial gut feelings. Her response also shows the dominant behavior of an extravert. She's not advising me on how to approach the issue, she's *telling* me what to do. "Say yes!" In my experience, an extravert will challenge you to take the next step. It's in their nature to want to influence the people around them. Whether or not their influence is positive depends on the relationship, and on their motives. You can influence people by being charming, showing faith in them, and encouraging them, just as you can do it by making demands and coercing them. Hanna has played a huge role in my own growth since I met her. She nudges me along.

This dominant trait isn't unique to Hanna; it's one of the core extraverted aspects. This is why most executives in the Western culture are extraverts. Sweden has an especially high ratio of extraverted executives. Organizations with a lot of extraverts are characterized by high levels of activity. Everybody gets involved in everything. Ideas aren't subjected to much critical thinking.

At the other extreme, an introvert can function as a kind of safeguard. We're the ones who explain to the extraverts around us that it's not a very good idea to use the toaster while you're taking a bath. We take a step back from things, maintain our distance to them, and think carefully about

146

what we're seeing. I'm convinced that these two approaches to decision making complement each other in essential ways. In a professional team, or in a relationship, we become each other's Yin and Yang. Cars need brake pedals every bit as much as they need gas pedals. In the light of this, I've developed a strategy for work where I actively seek out the people at the office who are the least like me. I've learned to enjoy working with people who are my opposite, because the things I hate doing are usually the things that this person lives to do, and vice versa.

Making decisions

My first question whenever I'm faced with a decision is always this: "How long do I have to think about it?" This can frustrate colleagues who want a quick answer, or life partners who want to know if you're going to agree to buying that new kitchen table.

Professor Frank Partnoy has studied the process of decision making. His decades of research can be distilled into this basic rule of thumb: *Never make a decision any sooner than you have to*.

The longer the thought process is, the more informed, objective, and rational your decision will be. In this extraverted day and age, we're often told how important it is to follow your gut feelings, and trust your own intuition. It's easy to allow your own pace to be dictated by the constant bombardment of media and information that we're exposed to, and make hasty decisions. According to professor Portnoy, immediate decisions are based more on emotions and hormones than on higher thinking. Quick decisions aren't usually based on *actual* problem solving; they tend rather to follow some precedent or template that we produce from our own mental archives. If we take the time to reflect instead, we'll allow ourselves to come up with a new solution instead of just recycling old blueprints. I've noticed that the answer often simply comes to us if we'll just give it time. The best solutions tend to appear out of nowhere, when I'm doing anything but look for them. Professor Partnoy claims that introverts' fondness for reflection aids them in their decision making.

One man's vacation is another man's hell

Have you ever thought about how different the things people choose to do on their vacations can be? Some people go for unorthodox spa treatments, and get their backs flogged with chives while listening to recordings of Tibetan bugle calls. A friend of mine spent five hours in a movie theater watching a Croatian independent film called *Darkness of the Human Soul*. People like him find peace in low levels of activity.

Others go Grizzly-watching in subzero temperatures, or go kayaking among killer whales on the open sea. They willingly board rusty old helicopters flown by hardcore alcoholics.

All of the activities above are thought of as *vacationing* by somebody or other.

Imagine you were leaving work to go on vacation for five weeks. What would you choose to do? A bunch of bearded psychologists studied the life patterns of introvert/extravert couples. Their conclusions are very indicative of the tug-of-war that goes on in relationships of this kind. They realized that we seek out different things when we feel good.

When an extravert is on top of things, it makes her want to do *more*. She wants to be even more active, climb even further, and meet even more people. And so, happy extraverts fill up their calendars with lots of activities. On the other hand, a happy introvert wants to relax, and *eliminate* activities from his planner. This is something that's come up a lot in my relationship with Hanna. When we

148

have free time, she plans things for us to do. Doing this makes sense to her, but I find myself longing for the gaps in between these activities instead.

I realize this can sound like a difficult situation. The way to balance it out is to make sure that both parties respect each other's needs, and to avoid having one person dominate the situation. *We* decided to go for a weekend trip, and *I* agreed.

Gifts

After school, the time came for me to decide what I would do with my life. I decided to be an illustrator, and I approached this goal the same way any introvert would. I sat down at the drawing desk that I'd built for myself, and began to practice. I'd made my decision, and I was determined to succeed. It turned out to be more difficult than I'd expected. Weeks turned into months, and months turned into years. I read about different techniques, and studied the artistic craft on my own. In time, I learned a lot about its various technical aspects. I also came up against some killer competition. In financial terms, I was living just above subsistence level. But I didn't mind. Money has no effect on my motivation. The people who were close to me all agreed that I'd be better off getting a real job instead of living with my head in the clouds. I remember a particular event that occurred during this time. One day, my father, who's probably one of the most introverted people on the planet, turned up at my place unannounced. He's an observer; the kind of person who doesn't say many words during a conversation. We've never discussed our dreams, emotions, or anything else of the sort. Sometimes, words are unnecessary. He'd decided to go out and buy me a whole set of oil paints and brushes. The gift itself wasn't important; what mattered was that he did it to show me that he approved of my choice of career. It was a silent gesture that spoke volumes. This is how introverts

149

usually reveal their feelings: not in their words, but in their deeds.

We all receive a large number of gifts during our lives. Some of them are great, and some of them are last-minute purchases from the gas station made by people with bad memories and guilty consciences. When a gift is from the heart, it's always great, irrespective of what it cost to buy. When we have good intentions, we give people things that we'd like to receive from others.

I've found it interesting to ask people this question: "What's the best gift you've ever been given?" I've thought a lot about the answers I've received. Extraverts tend to mention experiences, like parachute jumps, salsa classes, diving certificates, or golfing lessons. Things that have emotional significance, like friendship bracelets or name tattoos, also come up a lot. Introverts mention *objects*. A nice watch, an article of clothing, a record, or an e-reader – that sort of thing. The things that *everybody* seems to appreciate, regardless of their social preference, are surprise parties and great meals.

Are we tasting wine or making friends?

Hanna and I finally got to go on a date after a number of strenuous weeks, when our toddlers wouldn't sleep at night, and we both had to spend long days at work. We went to leave the kids with their grandmother, and headed off to spend some quality time, just the two of us. We'd signed up for a wine and cheese tasting that evening. However, the focus of the event wasn't quite what I'd expected. The first thing that happened was that we were expected to mingle with the other guests. I had thought of this evening as a chance to spend some time with my wife, so I was a little bothered by this. After the mingling, we were seated next to talkative couples at a long table. Having to concentrate on conversing and experiencing flavors at the same time overloads my system. I can literally feel my stomach tie itself into knots if somebody delivers an intense monolog to me while I'm eating. Therefore, the heavy emphasis on socializing, which I hadn't counted on, was mostly a source of discomfort for me.

I was sitting next to people who'd all decided that this evening was a great opportunity to make some new acquaintances. Unfortunately, my wife happened to be one of them. It's only natural for extraverts to want to turn strangers into friends. Introverts focus on developing the relationships they already have instead. Bus drivers, hairdressers, and strangers in elevators are all just props to us. Hanna and I had very different expectations for that evening.

Learn first, then unlearn

I think we tend to complicate ourselves as we grow up. When we're children, we hang out in the most natural of ways. A friend and I would sit together for hours, drawing in silence. Although our needs are the most natural things in the world, we tend to forget them. When we grow up, we often adapt our behavior to various social norms. We begin to follow specific rules of etiquette in our interactions with others, even if they make us uncomfortable. As teenagers, we hang out with the TV on, but we stop doing that when we get older. We've learned that it's not polite, and that we're expected to interact in a more adult and direct fashion. If you turn off the TV, you can focus better on the person you're speaking to, and this is thought to be considerate. I like having the TV on when there are other people in the room. I don't mind if the volume is turned down low, but I like having it there, so I can catch my breath when the social interactions get too intense. A good example of this is when somebody tries to lecture me about their political convictions. I think it's important to take a breather now and then, and ask yourself if what you're doing is what you *really* want to do.

Regardless of whether you're an extravert, an introvert, or an ambivert, it's up to you to do the things that make you feel good. It's realistic to expect to have to compromise from time to time, but I think it's important to differentiate between *voluntary concessions* and acting like a doormat. My main challenge as an adult has revolved around trying to find my way back to who I was before I became who I am.

When introverts hang out

How tiring an interaction is for an introvert isn't a matter of how long it goes on for, but of its nature. I can count the number of times I've gone out clubbing on the fingers of one hand, and the number of concerts I've seen on the fingers of the other. Those things simply don't appeal to me at all. It's unfathomable to me why anybody would want to pay 200 dollars to see Madonna perform in an overcrowded arena. I wouldn't even go if somebody paid me 200 dollars to do it. I'd rather have a wisdom tooth pulled than go to a book fair.

Here are a couple of experiences I've had that have resounded particularly strongly with my introverted nature:

The spring of 2003

My Spanish friend Sara brings me along to see the nightlife of Madrid. She's one of those people who's always smiling, and she has the most enormous afro I've ever seen. She's a warm-natured, impulsive person, and an extravert to the bone. She seems to know every single person who lives in this bustling metropolis. We make our way to a dark little club, where mellow jazz music permeates the smoky room. It's crowded, but I have plenty of space to lose myself in the music. We don't talk much; we mostly just take in impressions and sip red wine. Even though the place is so full of people, I'm buzzing with energy when we stumble out of there just before dawn.

The winter of 2005

The snow is piled up on the window-ledge. My partner at the time is working the night shift for several days running. I'm alone, or rather, I'm enjoying my solitude. I'm in my office drawing. A whole night goes by while I drink red wine and listen to jazz. Miles Davis plays on repeat. The thing I remember most of all is how my perception of time changes as I immerse myself in my drawings.

Some activities work well for everybody, regardless of their degree of extraversion. One example of this is people-watching from an outdoor café table next to a pedestrian walkway. An introverted artist I know often sketches people he sees on the subway train. One of my most extraverted friends likes to sit in the park and watch the people walking by.

Alone time

An introvert who's alone is in the best of company. As you know by now, it's very possible to be alone in a room full of other people, as long as you're able to do something that doesn't involve any intellectual or social interactions with others.

Alone time is something you need, not something you want. Like I explained earlier, it comes down to biology. Even most extraverts need alone time of some kind or other. If you're having a hard time understanding this need, try turning it around: what would it be like for you if you were completely cut off from all other people?

After we became parents, my need for alone time became quite pressing. It had never been a problem in the past. Whenever I felt like it, I could sneak off to work out, take a shower for an hour, or lose myself in a book. It didn't conflict with our lifestyle. While I was reading, Hanna would make a phone call, or go out for coffee with some friends. But suddenly, that freedom was a thing of the past. Our first time as parents involved a lot of anxiety. We tiptoed around, and constantly focused on the needs of our little miracle. It became almost compulsive. We got the idea that we shouldn't leave the house for any reason besides going to work. Parenthood became a ball and chain. We had to be present all the time in order to meet the insanely high expectations we had set for ourselves. I couldn't sneak off to the gym anymore; it would have felt like I was letting my family down. I couldn't stay up half the night writing, because our life was all about early mornings and lots of crying at night. I began to get desperate. My need for alone time was going unfulfilled. I felt guilty whenever I withdrew from them, as though I wasn't fulfilling my obligations to my family. It suffocated me. The thoughts I began to have made me understand how strong this need can be. I began to think a lot about what it would be like if we got divorced. Then, at least I would have alone time every other week. Fortunately, I chose to voice my concerns. No matter what previous generations may have thought, *passive-aggressive silence* isn't a very useful strategy in a relationship. These feelings were intensified by our long struggle to become parents. After the miscarriages, we felt that we should be incredibly grateful to be parents at all. We agreed to help each other find the time to do the things we need to do to achieve inner harmony, and we've stuck to this agreement. I spoke to a psychologist during this time. She said something that's been a rule of mine ever since. It's one of those truths that seem so obvious and trivial that we always seem to overlook them. She said: "Do what you need to do to get the energy you need to make a living. Otherwise you won't have any energy left to spend on other people." This is very good advice, no matter what your personality type happens to be.

I've discussed the need for alone time a lot with my closest friend. There seem to be some predictable patterns in place. Introverts tend to find their breathing space while the rest of the family is asleep. Dads will switch on their video game consoles after eleven pm, when the rest of the family are all tucked into bed. Moms will get up an hour before the rest of their family, to take a walk and gather their thoughts. There are all kinds of strategies for this. But it seems clear to me that this need is felt more strongly by introverts.

Beneath the surface

"Quiet people have the loudest minds"
Stephen Hawking

If you want to know what an extravert is thinking, you can simply listen and watch. If you want to know what an introvert is thinking, you'll have to ask.

I've realized that we can seem pretty mysterious to the people we live with. As a child, I hated it when people watched me while I was drawing. I found it incredibly distracting. My creative process depended on solitude. Once I'd finished a drawing, however, I was happy to show it to the people around me. It's the same way whenever I'm brooding over life and relationships. I don't want to talk about it until I've figured it out. Keeping one's thought processes hidden from the world in this way is characteristic of introverts. When we verbalize our thoughts, it's because we're done thinking. The danger here is how abrupt these developments can seem to our loved ones.

For instance, we might come to the conclusion that we don't want to stay in a relationship any more. This can be a shock to the other party, who never even suspected that we might have been unhappy. I've done this myself in the past, and I realize the devastating effect it can have on people. One day you're in a functional relationship, the next day you're packing your bags. The strange thing is that it's motivated by consideration for the other person. I don't want to worry my partner by telling her that I'm thinking of ending the relationship. After all, maybe I'm just going through a slump? It seems better to wait before saying anything. This is one of the true dangers of introversion.

I remember a tragic event that took place while I was growing up. A kid in my grade hung himself in his parents' garage. Nobody had any clue that he was depressed at all. From the outside, he'd seemed content with life. His grades were great, and he was a gifted athlete. But his family put a lot of pressure on him, and he was waging an internal war of emotions, which he eventually became a casualty of. Introverts have the unfortunate distinction of being far more likely to commit suicide. The fact that we don't talk about our feelings is part and parcel of our introversion, but it's also a choice we make. For some time, I've made a point of expressing my feelings. This has helped me establish closer relationships to the people around me. I'd even claim that this underestimation of the importance of emotions, our own as well as others', is an endemic affliction of introverts. Sometimes, even we don't notice that we're sad, because of the distance we maintain to our own feelings. Sometimes, we express ourselves in ways that others find cold or uncaring. On the whole, introverts are more sensitive than extraverts. Many introverts emphasize their own fear of conflict. We seek harmony rather than activity, and this is why we prefer to ruminate on things that are bothering us until we've figured them out.

Extraverts are often easy to understand, because they act out their personalities. They let people know how they feel and what they think. Even if you manage to get them to shut up for a moment, their opinions will be more than obvious from their body language and facial gestures. If an extraverted nightingale isn't happy, it'll simply refuse to sing. The expression "wearing your heart on your sleeve" is an apt description of these people's way of revealing their emotions. For this reason, these issues related to understanding tend to only go one way, and it's usually the introvert who's misunderstood. But it's our own fault. The effects of the behavioral norms of different cultures are both interesting and tragic. In extraverted nations (like the USA or Brazil) the number of homicides per capita is high. In introverted nations (like Finland and Japan), the murder rate is low, but the suicide rate is high.

Summary for extraverts

✓ Introverts enjoy stillness, and seek the absence of activities more than anything else. Therefore, an introvert's idea of a great vacation involves relaxation rather than adventures.

✓ Introverts are good at solving problems that they've never come across before, while extraverts excel at quickly solving problems that they've been trained to handle.

✓ Introverts have a strong preference for doing one thing at a time. We work efficiently when we're allowed to approach tasks in sequence.

The Power of Introversion

He took his time as he looked around the classroom. You could've heard a pin drop. Lars possessed a low-key charisma, which captivated the whole group of hormonal acne-ridden kids, myself included. It wasn't how he *spoke* to us; it was how he *listened*. We had lots of other teachers, but they were all authority figures who would preach to us with bloated confidence for hours on end, and never showed any interest at all in actually teaching us anything. They spoke to us as though we were sheep, and so, we didn't hear a thing they said. Lars was our history teacher, and his pedagogical approach was different. He would tell us a brief story, and then ask us open questions. When we answered him, he *really* listened. He spoke calmly, and quietly, but he still held our undivided attention. You don't need to be loud to make yourself heard. "Why did the Germans stay in Leningrad even after winter arrived?" He used pauses to catch our attention. Sometimes, he'd wait a long time for somebody to say something. He was comfortable with silence. He knew that somebody would answer him eventually. This was one of my first experiences of the power of introversion.

The strengths of the introverted personality go far beyond winning at Jeopardy or Trivial Pursuit. The statements below are taken from various scientific studies, and aren't part of some media blitz intended to condition you to accept that *introverts will rule the world.*

Earlier, I stated, somewhat cockily, that introverts are in the majority in terms of talent. What's that supposed to mean, and how can I make that claim? Most people would say that their personalities include both extraverted and introverted traits. If they're forced to pick a side, however, extraversion dominates by a wide margin. According to

Mensa, "while the general population is made up of approximately seventy-five percent extraverts and twenty-five percent introverts, the membership of Mensa is the nearly the reverse: approximately sixty-five percent introverts and thirty-five percent extraverts." In case you find this a little provocative, I'd like to add that I think introverts are neither superior nor inferior to extraverts. All I see here are two personality traits that we all possess to varying degrees, and that each bring their own benefits. In this chapter, I'll be focusing on the positive aspects of introversion.

Immunity to boredom

An obvious strength that introverts possess is our great tolerance for monotony. We fill our lives with content from within, thanks to our rich inner dialogs. Extraverts, on the other hand, find their inspiration outside of themselves. Studies have shown that introverts have a great capacity to endure boring situations. This tolerance for monotony explains why introverts tend to do well in the world of academia. Being stuck in your room with your nose in a lethally dull book is much more challenging for an extravert who's thirsting for some kind of activity. Introverts also need fewer breaks from work, as their natural state is one of great focus.

The mainstream vs. the road less travelled

It's been said that the foundation of our modern and open society was laid in 1955. This was when the flames of the revolution that's since become our own lukewarm everyday existence were first fanned. On a bus in the American South, a decision was made that would come to have far-reaching consequences. Rosa Parks, a diminutive lady of few words, defied the norms of her day by refusing to give up her seat to a white man, even though she was required to do so by law. Despite the mounting peer pressure from the other passengers on the bus, she refused to move. The situation escalated, and the police were called to the scene. She remained stubbornly fixed to her seat. The event took on greater proportions, and sparked a mass boycott of public transport throughout the US, which would eventually cause the segregation laws to be revoked. This event is thought to have indirectly caused the Great March on Washington and the Watts riots. Essentially, society as we know it today first began to take form on that bus in 1955.

Introverts' way of distancing themselves from groups can be a strength in certain situations. Extraverts prefer to act in collaboration with others, and to feel that they belong to the social network around them. For this reason, group processes will often have a greater influence on extraverts. Going against the group is costly when you put such an emphasis on belonging, and this is why extraverts can be so susceptible to peer pressure. Introverts, on the other hand, have a different sense of integrity, because we lack this need to belong to the group. I'd say that we'll often even seek to avoid things that are popular among the general public. Introverts don't evaluate different activities based on how popular they'll make us with others. We simply ask ourselves: "Do I like this? Do I want to do it?" Then, we act accordingly. We find excitement in things we haven't yet explored. Introverts often immerse themselves in things that seem niched, genuine, and original. Our interests are immutable, in the sense that we're unlikely to change our tastes to fit in. You could say that we feel loyalty to ourselves rather than to groups.

Security and risk aversion

Generally speaking, extraverts are more prone to taking risks than introverts, which also makes them more likely to end up in hospital. By nature, they have a great curiosity for exploring the world in the here and now; it's a basic drive of theirs. Since stillness isn't quite enough to keep them stimulated, they often have quite active lifestyles. They act first, and think later, rather than doing things the other way round. Sometimes, they don't even begin to think until they're already in a hospital bed. Statistics reveal that extraverts are more likely to suffer injury than us nerds. Accidental death is also slightly more common among extraverts. My daughter Smilla has her whole hand in bandages right now, after deciding to use it to explore the stove top.

There are historians who claim that some of the greatest mistakes in history were the results of rushed decisions made by extraverted leaders. A good example of this is the grisly tale of the Ford Pinto, which turned out to be a real fire hazard. It was rushed to market, despite having known structural flaws which could cause its gas tank to catch fire. This resulted in the deaths of several drivers. The original sales slogan for the car was quickly withdrawn: "Pinto, leaves you with a warm feeling."

The recruiter greeted me as I entered the room. She later told a colleague of mine that she had decided to hire me the very moment she saw me step through the doorway. It didn't matter much what I said, or what my qualifications were. Her decision-making process was immediate. This turned out to be a pretty unsuccessful recruitment decision, too; I wasn't suited for the job, and it didn't suit me either. This was the same recruiter who told me that her ovaries ached when we sat down to do the interview. She was a markedly outgoing and spontaneous person.

I know an experienced psychologist who's dedicated his life to providing leadership coaching to people who hold top-level positions in the world of business. He told me something that I found rather surprising, but the many tests and interviews he's performed over the years have made him quite certain of it. He believes that CEOs tend to be characterized by two specific traits. First of all, they're afraid of making mistakes, which causes them to focus on details, and the facts that are relevant to their decisions. Second, they approach the unknown with caution, i.e. they behave conservatively. These are clearly introverted traits. We often hear and see superstar entrepreneurs in the media, like Richard Branson of Virgin, who travels around the world in hot-air balloons and crosses the Atlantic in powerboats. Richard is an outgoing thrill-seeker. The fact that he's an extraverted entrepreneur has caused him to be given a lot of time in the spotlight. He's in the media all the time, and seems to have an endless supply of energy.

It's easy to think that people like him might be the norm among corporate leaders, because they outshine all the others in terms of media attention.

But is he really representative of corporate CEOs overall? Now and then, the market goes through a slump. When it turns downwards, introverted and extraverted managers handle the situation differently. An extravert responds to the change of circumstance by adapting her business. She'll take whatever actions she deems necessary. An introverted leader is more likely to try to weather the storm. She'll look over expenses, and manage the business in the same way as before, while waiting for the market to recover. As my friend the psychologist puts it: "So far, waiting for a better day has been a successful strategy." The darkest hour is just before dawn. This means that a conservative attitude can be beneficial in terms of long-term survival.

The downside to being positive

"I won!" Hanna yells, as she bounces up and down in front of her computer screen.

Having seen her behave this way before, I look up at her with a certain measure of pessimism. Her outlook on life is *positive*, which is a nicer way of referring to what an introvert would call *naive*. Somehow, Hanna has gotten the idea that placing the highest bid in an online auction is equivalent to *winning*. She's probably single-handedly responsible for around fifteen percent of eBay's total revenue. I usually tell her that what she's won is the privilege of paying more for something than anybody else was willing to.

This conversation is quite typical. Introverts are pessimistic, while extraverts tend to see things in a more optimistic light. They use a mental highlighter to mark up all the positives they can find in any situation. They trivialize problems and risks, like a bunch of Trojans admiring the nice big wooden horse they've just been given. This can sometimes seem quite provocative to a cynical introvert. But it can also be a strength, of course. Optimism is contagious, as they say.

I remember an exercise I once did in a management class. We were all given a set of drawing tools, and asked to draw a picture that represented our own self-image. Thirteen out of fourteen participants drew a colorful sun. I drew a blank face with a piece of charcoal. Later, when we discussed each other's pictures, the sun people all described me as "somebody who's out of balance with himself." I don't see it that way: I think being too positive is just as imbalanced as being overly negative. Sugarcoating every moment is simply play-acting. Not everything in life is sunshine, rainbows, and pixie dust. Being balanced, nuanced, and realistic seems to be the ideal state, if you ask me.

There are advantages to having a more cautious outlook on life. Being a little pessimistic makes you less likely to be disappointed, because your expectations are lower. Woody Allen once said: "I was walking around feeling so good about myself that I never realized how terrible I felt." A more objective outlook will also give you a more relaxed attitude to the decisions you have to make. Introverts are rarely in a hurry to make our minds up. Hanna often claims that making fast decisions, and not waiting too long before acting, is a virtue. And sure, it's true that the early bird catches the worm, but it's also true that the second mouse gets the cheese.

If you're gonna shoot, then shoot. Don't talk!

These words come from the classic western movie *The Good, the Bad, and the Ugly*.

They express a most interesting truth.

I remember something that happened a few years back. A girl I know decided that she would begin competing in Fitness, which is an extremely demanding sport, in both physical and mental terms. This girl had a very extraverted personality. She was covered in tattoos and piercings, and was always very cheerful and talkative. She was the kind of person who's always seen and heard, in any situation. She wore studs, glitter, and fluorescent colors, and put a lot of effort into standing out from the crowd. She proudly announced her intention in the coffee room. It's worth mentioning here that she was rather overweight at the time, and had very little experience of physical exercise. She made a big deal of throwing her burrito in the trash, and spoke long and passionately about what this would involve in terms of dietary changes, early-morning workouts, and so on. Her plan also included quitting smoking. We congratulated her on this life-changing decision, although my inner pessimist realized that we were praising her for possessing willpower that she hadn't actually displayed yet.

Then, her transformation began. She dedicated herself

completely to her training from that moment. Long before she'd even had any real results, she purchased a whole new wardrobe, consisting of nothing but sportswear. She bought herself whole a new lifestyle, and became very disciplined about bringing prepared lunches to work. She ate the meager fare of an extreme fitness diet: tuna fish, chicken, cottage cheese, that kind of thing. We obliged her when she sought praise, and showered her with compliments to let her know how disciplined, strong-willed, and plain awesome we thought she was. After a week, we'd chewed the topic of her great plans to bits, and moved on to discussing other topics during our coffee breaks. She continued doing her workouts and maintained her single-minded focus for a while, but she brought it up less and less. A few weeks later, there she was in the coffee room, eating a burrito again. The outlines of her cigarette packet showed through her hoodie pouch.

A long time passed before she even mentioned working out again.

She's in amazing shape today, which is why she agreed to let me share this anecdote.

There's an interesting psychological lesson to be learned from this story. It turns out that the more we speak about something, the less likely we are to actually do it. This has to do with how we respond to rewards. The more you talk about losing those forty pounds, the lower the probability that you'll actually lose them becomes. Why is this?

When you tell the people around you about your ambitious plans, they tend to react in a supportive way. Your friends, your family, and your co-workers will all give you love, praise, and appreciation, without demanding to see any serious effort on your part. You haven't lost an ounce yet, but you're already being showered with positive feedback. This is like receiving an advance payment on the rewards of achieving your goal. The more you talk about it now, the more of these advance payments you'll receive.

In time, you'll have diminished the value of the actual

reward to the point where achieving the goal doesn't matter much to you anymore. Motivating yourself to make the effort required for true success will become more and more of a challenge.

In this regard, I'd say that the reserve of introverts works out in their favor. Many introverts set goals for themselves without communicating them to the rest of the world. They tell people about it *after* they've succeeded instead. This is a very reliable strategy.

But there's another factor at play here as well: extraverts tend to have a positive estimation of their own ability to succeed, which causes them to set high expectations for themselves. Before a running race, for instance, extraverted runners are more likely than introverted runners to expect to make the top three. One effect of these expectations is that extraverts experience greater pressure than introverts do. The reasonable demands that introverts place on themselves are quite relaxing in comparison. These days, we're so convinced of the power of positive thinking that we tend to forget that there's another side to the coin. The generation that's growing up now has a greater belief in their own capacity to become anything they want than any earlier generation. One third of people born in the '90s expect to become celebrities at some point during their lifetime. A devastating majority within the same age group want to become entrepreneurs, and believe they can get rich quickly. In Sweden, seventy-eight percent of all teenagers say that they want to be in business for themselves. To contrast this with past generations, I'd like to mention a survey that Fortune magazine performed in 1949. Only two percent of teenagers back then could even imagine they would be running their own business. Young people today are very positive, and full of drive. But at the same time, this group experiences more stress than any other that's come before them. In the West, we've seen a spike in the use of psychopharmacological drugs among teenagers since the dawn of this positive millennium.

Positive thinking is a double-edged sword: it's good for your well-being to think positively, but positive thinking also means that you'll suffer more stress, because it makes you feel that the world is more available to you, which means that it's up to you to make all your amazing expectations come true. It's all in *your* hands.

"If you're gonna shoot, then shoot. Don't talk!"

Patience

A study was made in which people were led into a white, windowless room. They were left alone in there, cut off from every kind of amusement. They had no books, magazines, or other media. The walls were bare. The only thing in the room was a bunk. A voice in a loudspeaker instructed them to lie down and wait.

Of course, people can't just hibernate; they'll get restless sooner or later in a situation like that.

The study revealed a marked difference between the extraverted and the introverted test subjects. The extraverts were visibly stressed, and paced around the room much more than the introverts did.

I mentioned previously that one of the strengths of introversion is the tolerance for boredom that it gives you. In work situations, this means that introverts are able to focus longer, and delve deeper into their tasks. They don't need to take as many breaks, because this focus is already a natural aspect of their introverted personalities.

Living inside your head

It's like a warm wave that carries me to the computer. It's an urge every bit as powerful as hunger, sex, or sleep. This feeling only comes to me once I've set myself a goal. I need that vision of what I'm trying to achieve. Once I've made up my mind, my whole focus shifts to the target. I get impatient when I'm not at the keyboard. Not getting to write is like being stuck in a long bathroom line when you're absolutely desperate to go. The things going on around you get a little hazy. When I'm not writing, it's as though I was only half-listening to what people say. I get distracted. Later, when I'm sitting there writing, my focus can be almost frightening. The words gush forth from my fingertips, as though I was in some sort of trance. Pages fly by as I type my heart out. I lose touch with my body as I stare at the screen, and the minutes fly by. Hours pass, and I don't stir until something in the outside world breaks my focus. It's usually the phone.

I've always been this way. Psychologists have a word for this state: *flow*. Some people experience this feeling often, in all kinds of tasks. Others claim to never have experienced it at all. Flow is a journey *into your task*, whether it be writing, painting, singing, or something else entirely. Being an introvert means having a natural knack for attaining a high level of focus on what you're doing. When you need less stimulation, you're able to stick with the task at hand for longer, and keep going deeper and deeper until you reach a state of flow.

You can only achieve flow in activities that you've spent a lot of time on. Elite athletes often describe a perfect heat or a successful race in terms of flow, so this experience isn't limited to stationary intellectual pursuits. Flow is about performing well, with an extreme focus and genuine passion for something that you've invested a lot of time in. So far in my life, I can clearly remember experiencing flow when I've been writing, painting, or competing in the martial art of Wushu. I've done my best work in this state.

A number of people in history have exemplified the state of flow in various ways. One of them is author Alexandre Dumas, who experienced what he thought to be a trance state during his lengthy writing sessions. On one occasion, he's said to have written hundreds of pages of longhand without leaving the house. Flow is definitely a pleasant experience, but I wouldn't call it joyous; it's not as though you're sitting around laughing when you experience flow. Daniel Coyle, who's specialized in the study of gifted children, says that people who are experiencing flow are more likely to display a focused Clint squint than a smile. Flow involves withdrawing into yourself, and directing all of your mental capacity to a single task. You get tunnel vision, and it can take a lot to distract you when you're in this state. As I mentioned earlier, it's been suggested that introverts experience happiness differently than extraverts. I'd say that flow is one of the introverted aspects of happiness. Flow is when you experience a sequence of moments in which the task you're performing is its own reward. It's never about money. You can't force yourself to experience flow just because somebody hands you a stack of bills. Motivation is much more difficult to come by than that.

Many introverts have autotelic personalities, which make them better able to experience flow. The definition of *autotelic* involves lots of complicated jargon, but in brief, it goes something like this:

Autotelic person = somebody with a heightened motivation to undertake tasks. An autotelic person finds inspiration and pleasure in things that other people consider monotonous, tiresome, and strenuous. Not all introverts are autotelic, but it's a common trait among us. Perhaps you recognize these symptoms in your own behavior:

✓ Your thoughts are prone to getting caught up with stuff. Without quite knowing how it happened, you can spend half a party noodling away on a piano, playing Nintendo games, or reading about something you came across on Wikipedia. You seem to have a great capacity for being fascinated by everyday experiences.

170

- ✓ You have endless stacks of scribbled Post-it notes hidden away in various places. You often send messages to yourself from the supermarket checkout line, to make sure you won't forget an idea that suddenly came to you. Maybe you're one of those idiots who writes emails with one hand, and steers his car with the other? [1] Basically, you have a wealth of ideas, and you've learned that they disappear as suddenly as they came if you don't capture them in writing.
- ✓ You feel an indomitable need for the things you do to serve some clear purpose. You can't settle for a job where you're simply exchanging your time for money. You want to make a difference. You don't understand the concept of a nine-to-five job; all you can see is the task.
- ✓ From time to time, you're able to ignore your own needs almost completely, and fixate on the task at hand instead. You could be so hungry that your belly is howling at you, but you still keep telling yourself that you're just going to do *one more thing* before you go and have a bite to eat. There have been long periods of my life during which I basically subsisted on nothing but black coffee, dry toast, and flow.

I'm fascinated by all the little things that happen around me. Observing rather than participating is an aspect of introversion. I've always been captivated by visual impressions. Dramatic sunsets can have a hypnotic effect on me. This fascination also entails creativity and inspiration. Children are creative because they're easily fascinated. To a child's mind, every single thing you find by the side of the road could be useful for something or other. Kids are essentially hoarders at heart. Many people lose this ability to be fascinated by the little things when they grow up, and

---

[1] I feel I should take this opportunity to apologize to my fellow motorists.

don't see the beauty of an oil slick in a puddle any more. Adulthood sometimes puts blinders on people, closing them off from these kinds of experiences, and making them focus on mortgage payments, double glazing, and currency rates instead. If you ask me, these experiences of wonder take place in the inner world. Childhood wonder is a little slice of introversion.

Introvert and extravert creativity

Sometimes, people in creative lines of work talk about the four B's, which is a concept related to the issue of *where* we get our ideas. The four B's are places that seem to be more conducive to creativity than others: *bars, buses, beds,* and *bathrooms*. The fact that we tend to find the best answers when we're no longer looking for them is something of a mystery. When we relax, and do something else, the ideas we need seem to just appear out of thin air. If you have a problem that you're having trouble solving, go for a coffee break and wait. Most of my ideas come to me in bed. I very often get up again after I've gone to bed, because I need to write some idea or other down. Often, I'll have no idea what it was the next day, because of my horrendous handwriting (like many other introverts, I'm left-handed). It's often the same way when I wake up. The first thing that appears in my mind is something from my inner world, an idea that's been germinating while I was asleep. The brain is an amazing machine. As one might expect, introverts excel at producing ideas in solitude. It's important to understand that introverts need time to think; their best ideas are the result of unhurried reflection. Forcing a result in a busy meeting room is not a good strategy for us. Sure, we can meet to discuss the problem, but we prefer to withdraw into our cocoons afterwards, so that we can come up with a solution on our own, and bring it to the next meeting. Extraverts' creativity usually has more to do with what a team can produce through collaboration. There's been an astonishing amount of research done on creativity, which has produced astonishingly little in the way of results. Some studies claim that the idea-generating processes of extraverts are more conducive to innovation.

However, other research suggest that all creativity ultimately stems from alone time, and that introverted ideas and solitary thinking are the way to go. One particular theory about creativity presents an interesting notion: it assumes that nobody actually has the *whole* idea on their own. We carry lots of half-completed ideas around, and it's not until we come across the other half that we're able to see the whole solution. Extraverts often have large networks of contacts. They meet a lot of people, which increases their chances of finding the missing halves of their ideas. However, introverts have vast *networks of information,* in that we sift through a lot of information in books, reports, web pages, and media. We'll often find the missing half of our ideas there. This seems to imply that an optimally creative environment is likely to be a place where introverts and extraverts are brought together.

Some of the most creative duos in history were pairings of introverted and extraverted personalities. Two great examples from the world of music are Mick Jagger and Keith Richards of the Rolling Stones, and John Lennon and Paul McCartney of the Beatles. In business, the most obvious example is Steve Jobs and Steve Wozniak, who founded Apple together. Ted Hughes and Sylvia Plath are a good example from literature, as are George Burns and Gracie Allen from the world of television. The people in these partnerships are each other's opposites in many ways. The magic they created arose from the friction caused by their differences. As you might expect, these relationships are often quite tumultuous.

In Keith Richard's autobiography, he tells us of a time when their manager lost patience with Mick's and Keith's constant bickering, and literally locked them up in a room, and didn't let them out until they'd finished their song.

Creativity doesn't reside in harmony. A group of like-minded people is often harmonious; everybody understands one another, and any conflicts that do arise despite this are easily resolved. Decision making is easy too, because everybody tends to agree on what to do. Unfortunately, this isn't particularly fertile ground for new ideas. True innovation and creativity tend to result from a tug-of-war between strong wills with differing opinions. These conflicts produce new perspectives on things, which can pave the way to greatness. Try to include both introverts and extraverts in your teams.

I'm sticking to my core message here: both sides need to be represented.

The amusement park in my mind

Our senses aren't much to brag about in comparison with those possessed by some of the other species that live on this planet. There are birds that can see their prey from miles away in dim moonlight. Dogs can distinguish between the scents of millions of people. Blue whales communicate with each other through water, at distances of up to 300 miles. The distinguishing feature of humans is that we possess a sense that looks inward; we experience an inner world as well.

As an introvert, my strength, as well as my weakness, is my ability to lose myself in what I'm doing. This is a capacity I share with many other introverts. One of the gifts of introversion is the ability to turn impressions into images. We have cinema screens inside our minds, on which various episodes from different stories are projected. We're prone to turning our attention inwards.

As has been pointed out by some psychologists, this is the reason why introversion can be placed along the same spectrum as autism. Severe autism is exactly that: the inability to step outside of your own inner world.

I remember an exercise that we once did in a class I took. A number of us spent a few days working on personal development together. We took a personality test, and did lots of exciting exercises that were intended to reveal who we were. During this particular exercise, we listened to some instrumental jazz music. Afterwards, we were asked to tell the stories that we'd seen in our imaginations. What happened next amazed me.

I've never been in a conversation that was so dominated by the introverted participants, either before or since that day. Introverts seem to have lively imaginations, and this was plain as day on that occasion. There were sad stories about funerals, breakups, and betrayals. Somebody thought of the last days of summer, and a group of old people experiencing a sentimental class reunion. In short, the quieter participants had very vivid stories to tell almost immediately. I felt very at home in that situation. Show me a picture, or play me some music, and I'll find a story to match it, whether I want to or not. Many introverts are able to see hidden narratives in any picture. I think that seeing stories everywhere is a valuable gift. My imagination makes me happy, in a contented, introverted way.

Other people

Next, I'd like to address one of the greatest misconceptions about introversion: I don't dislike other people. In fact, I find most people to be interesting, sympathetic, funny, and talented. I just don't find interacting with them in a group context very interesting. I hardly ever call anybody just to have a chat. If I make a phone call, I have a clear purpose for it, which I'll usually state in three sentences or less. If I send an email, it's for a good reason.

As usual, I arrived in very good time. In fact, I was so early that I had time for a cup of coffee before my lecture. I googled "coffee" on my phone, and found what I assumed to be a café close to where I had parked. When I got there, something didn't feel quite right. There were no windows, just a big fire door and a modest little sign.

I knocked the door anyway, and an African gentleman came to open it. "Hi, can I get a cup of coffee here?" I asked him.

He flashed a big grin, and said: "This isn't a café, it's a roastery. But come on in, I was just going to make some anyway"

So I sat down there, in a room full of beautiful old coffee grinders from a century or so ago. He sat me down by a bar, and served me some gourmet coffee from Guinea.

I had a great conversation with this third-generation coffee roaster, who told me all kinds of stuff about coffee beans.

Many people believe that introverts don't enjoy talking to people. But that's not true. When somebody doesn't want to socialize, it's usually just because the situation isn't right for them (as in, there are too many people involved, and they're talking too loud).

A relaxed tête-à-tête, where you get to learn something new, can be truly inspirational. Spontaneous encounters of that kind are one of my favorite things in the world.

I like meaningful conversations, and I'm always up for a discussion, as long as it's actually going somewhere. Unfortunately, I find many everyday conversations vacuous and pointless. Outgoing people sometimes try to create a backdrop of unnecessary words. They like entering into a conversation just to find out where it'll end up.

Nobody needs to spend twenty minutes talking about the weather, or about what people they've never even met did on their vacation. My restraint isn't caused by some dislike of speaking as such. Rather, it's caused by my respect for the spoken word. For some reason, I feel that a person who's speaking has a certain responsibility to get to the point, without wandering off on irrelevant tangents. I also don't see any point in spending longer than necessary exchanging words.

If you sat down on a plane to Washington, and you were suddenly informed that the flight time had been changed to three hours instead of sixty minutes, you wouldn't just accept that. I feel the same about communication. Conciseness is a virtue. Because of this attitude, I often deliver my message quite quickly. Other introverts have told me they find it difficult to stretch their words out into a longer story. They tend to settle for a few succinct sentences. Many extraverts struggle with the opposite challenge: shortening their stories to make them less verbose. They use much of this *unnecessary* noise to form bonds with new people. There *is* a point to going on about the weather, the economy, or your aches and pains. These kinds of topics are called ice breakers for a reason. As a consequence of their conservative stance on small talk, many introverts end up with quite a small number of contacts in their phones, but they make up for this by enjoying very deep relationships with the people they do keep close.

Freud claimed that the greatest difference between introversion and extraversion has to do with self-control. According to his definition, an extravert is a person who doesn't show restraint, and is ruled by urges and impulses. Extraverts are more likely to be drug addicts, so maybe Freud was on to something. In one study of addiction, the conclusion drawn was that an addict's drug of choice would be determined by this aspect of personality. Surprisingly enough, people seem to prefer drugs that make them *less* like their social preferences. Introverted addicts often use crystal meth, which causes many people to become very outgoing and talkative. Extraverts tend to abuse opiates, such as heroin. One of the effects of heroin is a sense of great well-being, which eliminates one's capacity to experience boredom. This high is a kind of calm.

According to Freud, introverts are *people who show restraint*. He claimed that we have a more formal tone of voice, which raises a wall of sorts around us. This would explain why introverts so often shift back and forth between public and private personas.

Misused words

There are some words that require clarification. I've heard them all used to describe introverts at some time or other, but none of them actually apply:

Asocial. Somebody who lives outside of society's norms and rules. For example, criminals belong to this category. There's absolutely no connection between this and introversion.

Anti-social. This is a serious personality disorder, which is found in psychopaths. This has *no connection whatsoever* with introversion; it's used to describe people who lack all empathy for others.

Shy. Shyness isn't related to introversion or extraersion at all. It's the result of a predisposition to be uncomfortable with receiving attention. You could be terribly extraverted, and still be shy. What that would mean is that you would want to be around people all the time, but prefer to stay in the periphery of the group. Shyness is neurologically distinct from introversion. Here's a good way to think of it: if you're *afraid* of social situations, you're shy, but if you simply *prefer* to be alone, you're an introvert.

Unsocial. This describes somebody who has little or no interest in spending time with other people. This isn't connected to introversion, because introverts value relationships just as much as everybody else does.

A large study was made to investigate how social connections affect people. One of the most chilling conclusions is that the health-related effects of having no friends is equivalent to that of smoking fifteen cigarettes a day. This is true of both extraverts and introverts. Being an introvert isn't the same thing as being unsocial. It just means that you tend to prefer to interact with smaller groups of people, and relate to them in a deeper way. There's a one-liner I like that goes like this:

"I'm not anti-social. I'm pro-solitude."

Summary for extraverts

✓ An introverted disposition means that you tend to lose yourself in what you're doing. When this happens, you lose track of time, and the activity becomes its own reward.

✓ The introverted psyche comes with built-in pensiveness and caution. This makes us less prone to risky behavior than people who have more extraverted personalities.

✓ Introverts tend to be doers rather than talkers.

An Uplifting Upbringing

How to make or break talent

My math teacher in junior high school was many things, but *nice* wasn't one of them. His knowledge of the subject was solid, however. He'd stand at his desk and deliver his lessons, with a constant frown on his face and his pointer clutched in a tight grip. He explained something briefly, and then pointed at me.

"Did you follow that, Linus?"

"Um, yes", I nodded.

"Good, that means everybody else will have understood it to."

That's how he spoke to us. I hated him like I hated acne. He gave me a D. Then, a new teacher arrived; Roland, from Halland, the next province over to the North. Roland was a sympathetic and easy-going guy, who paid attention to each and every one of us. He'd soon established a relationship with all of the students in the class. When he addressed us, he spoke humbly. "Linus, I think you know the answer to this!" He was usually right. I would think for a moment, and then I'd know it. After one semester of math with Roland, my math grade had improved to an A. There hadn't been any change in my ability, but my interest level had improved enormously, and it was all thanks to my teacher.

Teachers, coaches and leaders all possess great power to help or hinder people. As a rule, the subjects that I enjoyed the most at school were the ones that we had the best teachers in. In one study, some of the best classical musicians in the world were asked to grade the teachers they'd had. Surprisingly enough, most of them felt that their teachers were more or less average, or even below average, in terms of their skill levels. What mattered was rather that these teachers were able to form good relationships with their students. When you've made a strong connection with a student, you can teach them something much more important than any technique: the passion for the craft.

A few years earlier, my gym teacher had said that it was a shame that I was no good with a ball. I'd never even reflected over whether or not I was any good with a ball. But the idea took root. My Swedish teacher, on the other hand, told me that I was a gifted writer, and that she thought I'd become an author one day. Since I'm only human, I did more of the things that won me praise, and less of the things that I was criticized for. Today, I'm one of the worst soccer players in Sweden, but I'll soon have published six books with three different publishers. I find myself wondering whether my life and my career would've ended up the way they did if it hadn't been for these people's opinions. I realize that many children are being shaped this way every day, in schools all over the world, and it makes me angry.

Many studies have been done on the topic of motivation. One distinction that's often mentioned is the one between *intrinsic* and *extrinsic* motivation. If somebody does something for money, that counts as extrinsic motivation. The same applies when something is done under duress, or out of fear: "I'll learn this math sum to make sure I won't end up being shamed the next time I'm singled out in class." There are different degrees of extrinsic motivation. For instance, doing something in order to acquire a certain identity is considered a case of extrinsic motivation: "I have to run the 60-yard dash in under 9 seconds, so that I can be on the school's athletics team like all of my friends."

Intrinsic motivation, on the other hand, is when we're motivated to do things because we find pleasure in them, or are passionate about them. When you do something out of passion, you're not thinking about monetary rewards. The state of flow is thought to be the strongest form of intrinsic motivation. Intrinsic drives are the best kind. When we're intrinsically motivated to do something, we'll remember information automatically, attain maximal focus, and feel that time is flying. Studies have shown that there's a connection between intrinsic motivation and introversion. Introverts generally act more on their intrinsic motives than extraverts do. We've discussed how flow is both a strength and a weakness of introverts. This means that our teachers have a huge impact on us. We learn to associate pleasure or danger with specific activities from an early age. I'd like to claim that a teacher like my old math teacher can cause any interested student to be filled with dread at the mere thought of mathematics.

Here's what I think: teachers don't need to motivate us; they just need to make sure not to discourage us. You see, the strange thing about motivation is that intrinsic motivation is fragile. It tends to be substituted by extrinsic motivation whenever the two are present at the same time. Here's a brief example of this:

Suppose you love to play football, and that somebody begins to pay you money every time you score a touchdown. Studies have shown that it's very likely that your love of football will be transformed into a love of the money you receive for scoring touchdowns. If your sponsor were to suddenly stop paying you, there's a good chance you'll stop playing football altogether.

Teachers, coaches, and leaders all have a significant impact on people's abilities to make use of their talents. These roles are key to all skill development, regardless of whether you're an introvert or an extravert. Albert Einstein summed up my feelings on the topic, as well as a remarkable amount of research into it, when he said that "it is the supreme art of the teacher to awaken joy in creative expression and knowledge."

Forcing introverted kids to conform to the extraverted norm

"Chuck's a bit of a wild one. He doesn't hesitate to lord it over the other kids. His kindergarten teachers tell me he's a bit of an alpha male." Chuck's dad's pride is evident from his posture. He can't help feeling a bit cool. After all, it's better to have a kid that pushes others around than the opposite, right? Extraversion and introversion lie at the core of our personalities, and can be observed early on in life. Most children at daycare show clear signs of having one or the other of these social preferences. Consider these questions:

- ✓ Do you want your children to know lots of other children, or would you be just as content for them to have just a few friends?
- ✓ Is it better for children to play outdoors, or sit indoors doing peaceful things like putting beads on pegboards, or drawing?

The norm these days is to prefer that your children be outgoing and active. We tend to regard the withdrawn and cautious children as somehow problematic. If our kids want to play on the PlayStation instead of going to soccer practice, we remember seeing those pictures of that 120-pound baby in China, and make them go. This has changed a lot since the '70s. The parenting ideal then was all about giving your children plenty of freedom to explore the world on their own. Children used to be allowed to spend their own time how they wanted, which made it easy for them to follow their own preferences. If they were active kids, they'd play football. If they were introverts, they'd settle down with a pile of comic books next to the record player. There was a huge shift in parenting trends during the 1990s. Parents began to take charge of their children's' agendas in a completely new way. They began to plan activities for their children, in order to encourage them to be active and develop their talents. This put greater pressure on the children to be active. Parents today work hard to balance out the complex logistics of driving their children to and from hockey practice, ballet, choir singing, orchestras, and horse riding. We rarely seem to consider whether we might be violating our children's personalities by doing this. I agree with Susan Cain's very astute observation: "Being an introverted child today is like being left-handed in a right-handed world." As recently as the 1950s, teachers would slap their students' hands whenever they saw them write with the "wrong" hand.

We're currently in danger of treating a whole generation of introverts the same way by teaching them that their personalities are somehow flawed.

We sometimes do the verbal equivalent of slapping our children's' hands: "You're not on that PlayStation again are you? Go outside and play with your friends instead." I think that it's mainly the introverted kids who feel pressured to live up to the expectations regarding activity levels in our time. They're already under enough stress, without having us add to their burdens. For instance, introverted children are more often bullied in schools than extraverted children. Stress is a major issue among children and teenagers in the Western world today. In Sweden, the use of psychopharmacological drugs among teenagers has increased by forty percent in the last ten years. A North American study revealed that the average teenager today suffers from the same stress levels as people who sought therapy for stress in the 1950s.

Seeing extraversion in children

This preference often manifests as courage. These are the kids who never seem to learn from their mistakes. They climb back up onto the armrest to balance on it again before the tears from their last fall have even dried. They soon grow bored of playing with things in the conventional ways.

Before you know it, they'll have invented some new death-defying way of riding the slide in the playground; head first is always a good choice. It's almost impossible to take a photograph of an extraverted child that doesn't come out as a ghostly blur. They aren't startled when a balloon pops at a birthday party, or when there's some scary villain on TV. They're curious about other people, and actively seek both eye contact and attention. Most of the time, they have a hard time playing on their own; they always try to involve somebody else in what they're doing. Handing them over to their grandparents for the night or leaving them at daycare isn't a problem. They find most activities exciting. They're present in the here and now, and alert to what goes on around them. An extraverted child will usually know exactly who gave them a specific toy or article of clothing. Their tempers are also very obvious and immediate. They show their anger, as well as their happiness, in unmistakable ways. They learn by doing, which is why they're usually covered in bruises, scratches, and Batman Band-Aids. Inventing imaginary friends is common among extraverted children. Sixty-five percent of all seven-year-olds have an imaginary friend, and this is an extraverted trait.

Seeing introversion in children

Introversion in children often manifests as a fairly stable mood, without the abrupt shifts that are so typical of extraverts. To some extent, these children are more easily frightened, and more sensitive to external events. They can start crying because of something they've seen on TV. But at the same time, they have independent personalities, and don't mind playing on their own for extended periods of time. Introverted children are often curious to find out how things work. Their thirst is intellectual rather than social. In other words, they're not necessarily any more tranquil than extraverted children, they just spend their energy on other things. A typical characteristic of introverted children is to prefer to observe new games first, before joining in.

Both of these types of children can be full of energy, but they use it differently. For instance, my daughter Smilla is a marked extravert, and she's always somewhere nearby myself or Hanna when we're at home. Whatever she's playing, she gets other people involved in it. Whatever she's doing, she demands attention. My son Ludde is more reticent. He can stay in his room for hours playing with his cars, without making a sound. This contrasts starkly with his sister, who always sounds like a Smurf on helium. Ludde puts his energy into exploring the world, and moving random objects from A to B, which is why I'm always finding my car keys in the trash, or uncooked macaroni in my jacket pockets. Occasionally, they reveal other aspects of their personalities. The other day, Smilla was sitting on a chair in the garden, looking a bit apathetic. It made me somewhat concerned, because of how far removed it was from my daughter's usual behavior.

"Aren't you going to play?" I asked her.

To this, my three-year-old answered, in an apathetic tone of voice: "I don't want to play. I just want to think."

It only goes to show that most people have both preferences to some degree. But no matter how much our children are pressured to be more outgoing, they'll remain the same on the inside.

That's why I'm convinced that trying to force children to behave in a certain way is a mistake. Constantly being told that they're not forward enough, or that they don't talk enough, can do harm to their self-esteem. It's like a wise person said: "If you judge a fish by its ability to climb a tree, it will live its whole life believing that it is stupid." Don't try to change introverted children, welcome the fact that they have other gifts instead.

My friend Annika remembers the summers she spent with her son when he was a child:

> We'd left the city, and moved to the countryside. I'd been imagining this idyllic life in the country, and I envisioned how my son would make friends with the other children in the area, and play with them all day long. They'd be jumping around on bales of hay, crab fishing, and riding their bikes everywhere. But my son just wasn't wired that way. He was fully content to spend time alone. He wandered around in nature, and enjoyed exploring the landscape on his own. One day, he came home and told me that he'd made three new friends. I could hardly conceal my excitement. "What fun!" I said, "what are they called?"

> He smiled: "Their names are Bessie, Clarabelle and Molly." My enthusiasm was somewhat dampened when I realized that these new friends he was talking about were three cows that he'd met.

If we travel back in time to revisit old memories, it becomes quite plain to us that we don't change much during our lifetimes. When I was little, I would wander away as soon as we walked into a supermarket. I felt secure about being alone, and I would soon get lost among the high shelves. More often than not, they'd have to announce my name over the PA.

The evolution of the teacher's pet

Outgoing students have taken over the role as model pupils in schools. I most recently noticed this when I lectured at the Procivitas high school in the south of Sweden. This a school that only admits students with top grades. I had an idea of what kind of kids I'd see in the auditorium when I walked in

188

to give my lecture. I knew what the geniuses had looked like back in my day. We're talking a body mass index of either 45 or 3, and the ever-present bowl cut. As I turned to face the audience, I wondered if I might be in the wrong school. Instead of kids with thick glasses, these were all attractive and fashion-conscious boys and girls. This is where the people who are good at arguing and negotiating end up. The nerd of yesteryear is all but extinct. It used to be that you could get good grades by scoring well on tests. You didn't have to give presentations, other than a shaky show and tell effort from time to time. We'd read from our notes, with trembling hands and monotonous voices: "The gerbil gestates for four months, and has four to seven pups per litter." That would never cut it today. Now, schools teach rhetoric, presentational technique, and negotiation. You need to be able to present arguments and debate on a completely different level. Today, there are standardized tests in which one of the assignments involves giving a presentation in the auditorium. School has become an arena for extraverts, and this has elevated the status of outgoing, sociable students who are good networkers.

The personality test

There's a riddle I'd like to solve. It concerns a picture which I'm so fond of that I've had it printed on the back of my business card. It's made up of a bunch of blotches and patterns of various shapes and sizes. When people look at it, the results are interesting. Most people just see a bunch of dots. They twist and turn the card every which way, and make some very amusing faces. But then there are some people who just glance at it casually for a second or two, and then immediately announce what it is.

It's fascinating to try to figure out why people see it so differently. Psychology is at a loss for an explanation. My own observation so far is that the ones who can see what it is are often quiet types. An acquaintance of mine has a five-year-old daughter who saw it right away. The people who figure it out are often peaceful individuals with somewhat bohemian lifestyles. They tell me what it is as though it were the most natural thing in the world. Sometimes, I'll tell a white lie, and tell them that the people who can see what it is immediately are usually introverts This has yet to be disproven, and it remains my own theory. This statement often gets quite a strong reaction. "Nooooo, don't say that!" the HR manager says, and wrinkles his nose so hard that his glasses almost fall off. Most people are very averse to being labeled introverts. It has negative connotations, as though it were some sort of social disability. Of course nobody wants to be somebody who *dislikes* socializing. To many, success essentially means that you have a large network, and are a familiar face to many people. By the way, the picture is of a

Dalmatian poking around among some leaves on the ground.

A woman I know is greatly opposed to the very concept of introversion. Like many others, she uses herself as an example of why the word doesn't make sense. She's an independent person; the kind who travels to the other side of the planet to philosophize and spend time alone. She spends her days people-watching and wandering alone through urban and rural landscapes. She's a productive writer, who publishes a new blog post every day. She spends a large portion of her time reading:

"That's nonsense. I'm an extravert; I just don't like superficial conversations. I prefer to have in-depth discussions with one person at a time." Despite everything I've told her, she remains determined to be the exception that proves the rule. She refuses to let go of her conviction that she's an extravert. I asked her if she was *really* sure, to which she replied that she'd been tested, and that her results showed that she was an extravert. "Who tested you?" I asked. "I did it myself. It was a self-assessment test."

This only makes the issue even more interesting. We're all *at least* three different people: the person we *want* to be, the person we *are*, and the person that *others* see us as. The problem with self-assessment tests is that we so commonly put so much of *who we want to be* into our responses. But at the same time, tests of this kind are maybe the best way we have of identifying our true personalities. My colleague is in good company. The general public takes extraversion to be the norm, and thinks that there's something inherently admirable about being outgoing.

Summary for extraverts

✓ Introverted children are often independent, but easily frightened. They prefer to observe a game before taking part in it.

✓ Introverts are intrinsically motivated to a great degree, in that what drives them is their love of the activity they're performing. Money and status have little effect on their motivation.

✓ In Western culture, our expectations regarding people's behavior often follow an extraverted template. Because of this, we tend to overlook the introverted aspects of our own personalities.

Introverts at work

The men in the funny hats dragged Ferdinand the Bull into an arena where he didn't belong. The people who did the same to me didn't wear any funny hats. They were the management team of a consulting firm, and they managed to convince me to leave my cork tree far behind.

I had a tingling sensation on my first day. I felt wound up. It was as though I was trying to fire myself up before entering this cutthroat environment. My boss had given me some pretty grim expectations when she described their corporate culture to me in broad strokes. She painted a picture of a business run by a bunch of ambitious, status-oriented sharks. The internal competition was tough as nails. The office floors were bustling with trend-conscious yuppies who had all graduated with top grades from the best universities. Things changed at an extreme pace, and decisions were made quickly and reactively. There were a lot of ruthless internal politics going on, with intricate webs of alliances and back-scratching. This was a fast-growing business, that was very strongly rooted in an extraverted culture. This was far from an optimal situation for me, but I somehow hoped that I'd be able to make a difference, and *create art* even in this place.

I put on my colorful suit and made my way into the world of IT consulting. I swallowed my introversion down deep inside, and became one of those glib types I'd always despised. In the daytime, I ran meetings, and used pretentious phrases like *synergistic effects*. I managed projects, managed networks, and communicated until I went blue in the face. My job often involved resolving conflicts between various parties. It's weird that an introvert like myself ended up being tasked with getting these extraverts to stop marking territory and begin talking to each other. Some nights, I would come home and sit through dinner in silence, with a thousand-yard stare plastered over my face. Then, I'd play video games until my fingers bled, and try to find some way to escape my own thoughts.

Falsification

This outgoing role simply didn't suit me at all. During this whole time, I was manic, stressed out, and confused about my own identity. Being able to be somebody else for a limited time is a strength. Having the capacity to reshape your own personality and behave in a more outgoing or introverted way than you normally would is useful, and serves some purpose or other in almost any profession. Even a job involving lots of social interaction will usually include some more typically introverted activities, such as administration or documentation. This is only natural. However, there's a serious danger involved in letting this strained mode of being become business as usual. If you get stuck in a role that just isn't you, it'll cause you harm sooner or later. Psychologist Katherine Benziger has studied this phenomenon, and named it *falsification*.

An introvert who's stuck in a professional role where she constantly has to be the center of attention in social situations is falsifying her personality. Benziger claims that what we refer to as burnout is mainly the consequence of a poor match between our personality type and our work situation.

Falsification is stressful for everybody, regardless of whether they're introverts or extraverts. There's no universal definition of what causes stress. It differs from one person to the next. For example, an introvert could be stressed out by a job where the goalposts keep moving. Having to travel to the other side of the planet with no more

194

than a day's advance notice would be a source of stress for most introverts, while an extravert might simply find it exciting. Extraverts are more likely to experience stress in working situations that are too predictable, where too much attention to detail is required, and where things don't change often enough. This is known as *boreout*, which is the opposite of *burnout*. Our needs vary, as do the sources of our stress.

As Benziger was studying people who were falsifying their personalities, she identified a range of remarkable symptoms that can appear. Individuals who falsify can have weakened immune systems, and seem to suffer from chronic colds. Their memory is impaired during their falsification, and they suffer sleep deprivation. Many people report that their stress manifests as difficulties falling asleep at night. Benziger recommends that we find roles that allow us to spend at least half of our time doing things that suit our temperaments.

Introversion and extraversion are aspects of our identities. My opinion on career choices is that it doesn't matter if everybody in your family is an accountant; who you are in this respect is simply a biological fact. Therefore, you should choose a professional role that suits the person you are deep down.

So what makes a good leader?

If you ask an organization what characterizes a good leader, they'll hit you with more clichés than an infomercial for a piece of exercise equipment. A good boss is *committed*, *creative,* and *driven*. These traits aren't exclusively extraverted or introverted as such. If we examine how these traits are expected to *manifest*, however, a clearer picture emerges. I posed this question to a woman who works as a recruiter for a large tech company. I asked her to elaborate on the meanings of each word.

195

Here's what she associated with being *driven*:

"Being optimistic, and seeing opportunities everywhere! A driven person is forthcoming, and not afraid to speak her mind. She doesn't hesitate to deal with conflicts when the need arises."

This is how she described the meaning of *creative*: "A creative leader is able to utilize everybody's individual skill sets to make progress. He realizes that everybody is smarter than somebody else in some regard."

She described *committed* as follows: "Committed people do their jobs from the heart, rather than out of a desire for money. You can tell when people have commitment," she says, with fire in her eyes.

"How can you tell?" I ask.

She answers immediately: "It's a kind of restlessness, like when somebody stands up to speak on the phone, and can't help leaking energy, and moves about a lot. People who have commitment speak loudly, and spontaneously, and their behavior affects others. They're able to get people onboard with them. Their body language is often loud, and they don't try to hide or apologize for their commitment. A person who has commitment likes to be the center of attention!"

I sat there in silent thought as her words drifted towards the periphery of my attention. It seemed to me that what she was describing was actually *extraversion;* more specifically, the extraverted version of commitment.

A colleague of mine studied literature at university, and did so with enormous focus and genuine commitment. He once read two thousand pages of fiction in a week. He isolated himself from the world completely, and unplugged his phone. If you ask me, *that's* an incredible manifestation of commitment.

I've just written two hundred pages over a period of three weeks. Even though I've been sitting still a lot, I consider this to be an act of both self-discipline and commitment. But it's not the kind of commitment that *makes itself heard*. My commitment is nothing like the kind of commitment that the recruiter described. Sure, taking part in corporate events, kickoffs, and business networking is one way of showing commitment. This is something introverts struggle with. A night out with the company usually follows the same pattern: tradition dictates that you dress in formal, uncomfortable clothes, and visit various establishments in the company of formal, uncomfortable people. The night begins with a compulsory mingling session. You talk about the weather, mortgage rates, or the Super Bowl. Most of your colleagues appear to be quite uncomfortable with this as well. You realize that you're spending a night of your personal time on superficial interactions with your coworkers, and doing stuff that you don't enjoy. Participation in these events is thought to be a sign of loyalty and commitment. Some companies have begun to take attendance during these events. If somebody's absent a few times in succession, they'll be flagged in the HR systems, to indicate that they're likely to leave the company before long. I think this is a ridiculous way of measuring people's passion and commitment. Many introverts will gladly trade away lots of private time in order to achieve some result or other at work. We don't mind spending late nights at the office, with nothing but Snickers bars and instant coffee to keep us going.

We find champagne pyramids and that sort of thing much more taxing than actual work. Contributing to a positive atmosphere is definitely a way of showing commitment, but so is spending your evenings and weekends finalizing patent applications, even if this is commitment of a different kind. Introverted commitment is a silent force of nature. This is an obvious weakness in a world where the volume of your voice is often what determines your success.

The contemporary ideal for a *perfect leader* doesn't seem to recognize any of the more withdrawn qualities – if you're not being heard, you don't exist.

If you're the thoughtful and reflective person at a corporate meeting, this will often be interpreted as a lack of

197

interest or initiative on your part. Acting immediately, with conviction, is considered a strength.

During a performance review, my boss asks me: "Your demeanor is quite reserved. How can we activate you?" Without thinking, I reply: "I'm not a Tamagotchi. You don't need to activate me."

Because I move in circles where issues like these get discussed, I've arrived at the conclusion that these ideals vary somewhat from one company to the next. In the West, we have a culture of risk taking. "It's better to try and fail, than not to try at all," or at least that's what all those chipper leadership coaches in pinstripe suits keep telling us. "It's better to apologize than ask for permission" is another cliché that you'll hear somebody or other say at every single corporate meeting. I believe in balance: we need both the gas pedal (optimism) and the brakes (risk evaluation). Today, the state of the economy seems to have put our car in neutral and sent it rolling down the steepest hill in the world. This risk-taking perspective is especially strong in Scandinavia; this is a culture where we believe in taking risks. Perhaps this has something to do with our great welfare system, and the fact that everybody knows that they'll be OK even if they go bankrupt? But this brings us back to our question: What *really* makes a good leader?

And the winner is...

The Myers & Briggs Foundation has collected information about people's introversion and extraversion since the Second World War. By now, their database contains hundreds of thousands of test results. This information is interesting, because it can provide answers to a number of different inquiries. For instance, you can find out which professional roles have the largest proportions of introverts.

Studies of leadership have been made in which analysts sifted through this database carefully to determine which personality type is best suited for leadership roles. Their conclusion is surprising to many. Among leaders, the different personality types are fairly evenly represented. It turns out that you can be a successful leader regardless of your social preference, and that your level of success depends on a different trait altogether. Their conclusion was that what separates the truly successful leaders from the rest is their degree of *flexibility*. An introverted leader who's highly flexible can adapt to situations involving large groups, and make his case even in contexts that he might seem ill-suited for. In the same way, a good extraverted leader is able to step back and let others take the floor. Studies of leadership emphasize that introversion and extraversion are both desirable traits in a leader.

Introverted leaders are good at managing independent employees. Extraverts often function better as managers of work forces that like to be given orders.

The ability to socially influence others is one of the reasons why extraversion is often associated with leadership. It's important not to overlook quiet leaders, who can definitely be forces to reckon with. Gandhi was an introvert. So were Martin Luther King and Rosa Parks. This tells us something about commitment and leadership. After all, these are the people who caused some of the most monumental upheavals in the history of our civilization. Introversion has nothing to do with a lack of passion. If you step on something that an introvert cares about, you'll soon know how hot their fire can burn.

Introverts and extraverts have very different ideas about what makes an *ideal boss*. Extraverts tend to want to work for somebody you can talk to, and are free to disturb at any time. Their ideal boss keeps an open door, and is always available for creative and personal discussions.

An introvert's ideal boss is more likely to be somebody who delegates well, and in the right way. This means delegating entire areas of responsibility rather than individual tasks. The more clearly defined the task is, and the greater the freedom is to work within that definition, the easier it'll be for us to go off and work independently on it. We like to isolate ourselves and lose ourselves in what we're doing; it helps us perform at our best. A good boss is somebody who doesn't micromanage, and can state the desired end result clearly.

The more freedom we have to plan our own time, the greater our commitment to the task will be. If I was working as the leader of introverts, my first step would be to abolish compulsory meetings. Let them work as independently as they need to. Introverted leadership evidently has its strengths: Queen Elizabeth II has served as monarch for more than sixty years, and has uttered about twenty words throughout her career.

However, the notion that introverts don't appreciate praise as much as their extraverted colleagues is simply ridiculous. It's completely incorrect, but I can see how our lack of expression might make it seem that way.

A very interesting piece of the leadership puzzle was clarified in 2010, when the Harvard Business School published an article based on a number of different studies of leadership. In it, they showed that introverted leaders are an especially good fit for independent and proactive co-workers. Among the mentioned advantages of introverted leaders was the fact that they "don't monopolize speaking time" during meetings, and that they allow differing opinions to co-exist within the group, which boosts creativity.

Details aren't details to people who care about them

I can usually spot him long in advance. There's always at least one of them in the audience. He sits quite far back in the room during my presentation. After the lecture, the people who want to ask further questions gather up front.

First, the banderilleros approach me. These are the exuberant extraverts, who want to tell me about any experiences they might have had that are in any way related to what I spoke about: "My daughter is just like the people you described, and she ..." They like to talk. Next come the picadors, who have questions to ask about the content. "Everybody on my team is a millennial. How should I do so and so..." These people want to listen. He waits patiently while all this is going on, and maintains a blank expression throughout. When everybody else has asked their questions, he approaches me, brandishing his smartphone. "I couldn't help noticing something you said before: Monty Python released *Life of Brian* in 1979, not 1978 like you said." This man chose to spend thirty minutes waiting just to correct me on this single fact.

Perhaps the strangest thing here isn't that he did this, but that I appreciate the gesture. Having the right facts means everything to me, which is something that's quite typical of introverts. We can be quite fanatical about details. It's as though we have to fit everything we see into the right structure and system.

A woman who read my first book emailed me a list of almost 200 corrections that she thought I should go over. Of her own accord, she had decided to mark up every single place where there was a space missing, or a superfluous space that needed to be removed. The fantastic part was that she did this while she was reading a book that had already been professionally reviewed, and was already available in stores. This kind of eye for detail is a fantastic gift, and a true talent. I'm very grateful to her for investing so much time in doing that, and when I asked her why she had, she simply responded that the typos had disturbed her sense of order.

I once found the following brief message on the letters page of a Swedish magazine. I suspect that the sender was an introvert:

> *In regards to the July issue: there was an 'f' missing on page 45, line 5, in the 3rd word, as well as an 'S' on page 57, line 2, in the 7th word.*

Structural obsession is another trait that's related to this appreciation for detail. My constant catchphrase whenever I'm watching a movie is: "Where have I seen that actor before?" Then, I'm *completely unable* to let it go until I've looked up every movie this person was ever in. It's like a kind of obsessive compulsion, or a mental tic. I can't concentrate on the plot at all until the matter is resolved.

Job fairs

When companies want to meet new talent, they get a booth at a job fair. These events usually take place in large venues, where thousands of visitors from different colleges gather to rub elbows and eat lots of free candy that nobody really seems to like. It's like a speed dating session, in which slick business students get short of breath trying to promote themselves to corporate representatives who look like they spend half their time on tanning beds. They students are expected to describe themselves in a way that's ideally a little funny, very impressive, and most of all exciting – all in a few seconds! Most of them sound exactly the same as everybody else. The company reps counter by saying something about the company that's a little funny, very impressive, and most of all exciting. They all sound the same as well.

In this situation, the talents are expected to make connections with the companies, and sell themselves to them as though they were products. It's hardly surprising that this isn't an environment that attracts hordes of introverts.

In my region, there's a well-known network in place for connecting young talents with established businesses. What they do is meet in large groups, and have round-table discussions and Q & A sessions. This also favors extraverted job seekers quite heavily. In this situation, you need to be spontaneous, expressive, and convincing. These events aren't suited to the kinds of talents that are typical of sharp introverted intellects.

However, some companies have figured this out. You won't find any introverts on an indoor football field full of noisy booths. We like to speak to one person at a time, and find inspiration in things that appeal to our intellects. There's a fun event called *Robotics*, which is organized by a consulting firm in the south of Sweden. Here, people get together to program robots, and then proceed to let them duke it out in a digital world. You could mistake this event for a Mountain Dew drinkers' convention. It's a gathering where introverted stars receive a lot of affirmation.

I saw an interesting want ad, which was obviously designed to attract introverted talents:

> *We're seeking systems developers with advanced programming skills.*
> *Call us at: x 24, y = 30 Phone: = 01.$(y^2$-x$).(y^2$-$10^2)$x10*

I like myself

There have been a number of studies made into how candidates are evaluated in recruiting situations. Most recruiters decide how they feel about a candidate within the first four minutes of an interview. It's worth knowing that we tend to recruit people who are like ourselves. It's quite logical: we like ourselves, and we find our own values to be sound. It's only human to look for people who reflect our own personalities in this way. The thing that can cause an imbalance here is that most of the people doing the recruiting are extraverts. This is hardly strange, as they dominate the planet anyway, and like to talk to people, which is why they're attracted to recruiter jobs in the first place. Who does this benefit? Extraverts, because they'll mirror the recruiters better than the introverts will.

Multi-dimensional talents

One lady towers over everybody else in this open office space. She's tall, has great posture, and is very intense. Her voice cuts through the rows of desks as she casually conquers the world one phone call at a time. Hers is a very particular kind of charisma, a bit like a 1,000 Watt light bulb. She shines so bright that she's guaranteed to get your attention, at the possible expense of blinding you. Her strategy is every bit as unique as it's brilliant. Her name is Linda, and she's a sales superstar. When she calls clients, she overwhelms their defenses with a tone of voice so sincere and positive that they can't help but be curious to know more. She's as spontaneous as they come. She sometimes sings to her clients on their birthdays. Her sales calls are long, but her hit rate is phenomenal. Some days, she wears a cowboy hat to the office. Like any strong personality, she divides the world into two categories: people who love her and everybody else. She straddles the line between insanity and brilliance. She's a salesperson through and through, and an extravert without equal, with an almost supernatural ability to influence others.

Let's look at another workplace. Imagine an office space where there's nothing but endless lines of desks, as far as you can see. This place has a younger sales force, and its culture is much more competitive. They've squeezed a huge number of great egos into all of these little desks. The people here are trendy, confident, and always on the move. We're talking upturned collars, orange skin tones, perfect teeth, and an ethos defined by ruthless ambition. This team makes sales calls all day as well. The competition is brutal, and the performance indicators aren't very forgiving of weakness. Each week, the performance of every worker is summarized and quantified, so that they can crown a king or queen of the self-proclaimed smooth-talkers. The strange thing is what happens every week; one of the members of the team practically subscribes to the gold medal. This girl is the undefeated heavyweight champion, who wipes the floor with all the other salespeople, despite her slight build.

If you spoke to her, you'd most likely be surprised. She's nothing like the cocky, colorful self-promotion machine you'd probably be expecting.

You'd notice that you were speaking to a quiet person, who makes a very modest impression. She's an introvert, with a relaxed demeanor that the people she speaks with respond well to. There's something about her calm that instills trust. Her customers are convinced that this person they're dealing with won't give them the hard sell. They feel secure as she objectively and succinctly advises them on the various options open to them. She never uses slogans, clichés, or obvious sales pitches, and the people she speaks to don't have to fend off some avalanche of words or sycophantic jargon. Her communication is based on direct and sincere dialog.

However, there's a great deal of energy hidden just beneath the surface here: a silent, introverted primeval force. She doesn't convince people with the words she says, she convinces them with the things she does. In her own mind, she's figured out exactly what she wants to achieve, but she doesn't tell anybody about it. Not telling people about your goals, as we discussed previously, is a strategy that has very powerful psychological effects.

The thing that makes her such a sales ace isn't how she talks to her clients; it's how she listens to them.

A professor named Adam Grant performed a large study that revealed something many people have had a hard time believing: that extraverts tend to be terrible salespeople.

According to his study, ambiverts are by far the best at this task. They have an easy time finding the right balance between listening and speaking. In his study, which included just over 300 salespeople, the ambiverts performed the best by a wide margin, making 32 percent more money than the extraverts. The silver medal went to the introverted salespeople, and the extraverts came in last. Personally, I believe that extraverts did better in sales before the last decade or so. In recent years, many consumers have become experts at critically evaluating information. We use the Internet, and different price comparison services. We make our decisions when we're out of the aggressive salespeople's reach.

That being said, I'd like to emphasize something I've noticed. We often have preconceived ideas about how somebody ought to act to achieve success within a particular profession. For instance, we tend to associate extraversion with sales, management, teaching, and tour guiding. In similar fashion, we think of programmers as introverted button-pushing chimps, who live in their cubicles – a real-life quote from one of my previous employers. A recent Cuban study of computer programmers actually revealed that most of them are extraverts. Extraverted developers are successful because they can utilize the skills of the entire team, instead of having them all try to solve everything on their own.

Generalizing might not be dangerous, but it can often cause us to make mistaken assumptions. Just like in the examples above, there are people of both dispositions who manage to make their personalities work really well for them. The girl in the second example wouldn't have made it to the second round if she was applying for a job as a sales superstar, since she doesn't exemplify the personality type most people expect to see in that role. The conclusion to be drawn here is that personality has no bearing on competence in most jobs. Focusing too much on the specific character traits of candidates can cause us to overlook some amazing talents.

Summary for extraverts

✓ Exceptional leadership isn't a matter of introversion or extraversion, but rather one of taking responsibility for a situation. Flexibility is a common characteristic of skilled professionals in general.

✓ In business, introverts can sometimes be thought to be lacking in motivation because of their limited participation in after-hours social events. Conferences and gala dinners aren't an introvert's idea of a good time.

✓ Introverts often have a great sense of detail, which makes them very well-suited for quality assurance work. If the material has been reviewed and approved by a number of introverts, it's very likely to be a solid piece of work.

What's the Best Working Environment, and the Best Kind of Leadership?

Open plan offices are the worst

"OK, let's do this!" You crack your knuckles over the keyboard. It's time to focus! You have to write a full report on the project you've just finished. Three seconds into your writing session, an outrageously annoying ringtone goes off. The phone lights up, howls and vibrates on the third desk down, where its owner must have left it. Eventually, it goes quiet again. You lower your eyes. Somebody starts laughing like a deranged hippo in another part of the office space. You close your eyes, and begin trying to rebuild the collapsed house of cards that is your thoughts. A group of people who are speaking in the most horrendous accent known to man kick off a brainstorming session at the far end of the room. You try hard not to listen, but their words penetrate your skull, consuming all of your attention. The man to the right of you clears his throat and coughs for the thousandth time this last hour. This guy decided to come in to the office even though he's obviously contracted Ebola. His dry, rattling cough makes your skin crawl. The woman across from you is so into the music that's leaking quite audibly from her headphones that her chair squeaks as she moves back and forth while listening to it – and to make things worse, she's clicking her ballpoint pen to the beat as well. Behind you, somebody's breathing loudly through his nose as he reads. You're surrounded by noises and distractions. When open plan offices were first introduced, they were said to boost creativity and collaboration, but the only thing that's getting boosted here is your stress level.

You give up, and accept the fact that you'll simply have to write the report when you get home, where you'll have the peace you need to concentrate. To get here, you had to spend an hour on a crowded commuter train, crammed in between rain-soaked people who smelled like ash trays. You had to go to all that trouble just to get to a place where you can't get any work done. When the introvert revolution comes, the open plan office will be its first victim. Open plan offices are to work what chicken steak tartare is to fine dining.

Putting people in huge open plan offices has been an increasing trend in business over the last few years. The only sanctuaries that remain for agoraphobic introverts are the small rooms that are really intended for phone calls. That's where we go whenever we need to get some work done, to seal ourselves off from the eternal coffee break outside. Since the 1970s, the average space per worker has been cut in half. The majority of all office work today is done in open plan offices. We keep squeezing more and more people into ever shrinking floor spaces, while demanding more and more sophisticated results from them. Surely this can't be the best approach to work we can come up with after all those millennia of evolution?

The idea of an open plan office is something that could only appeal to extraverts, and only if they were feeling generous. Studies of stress have shown that introverts are far more sensitive to distractions than extraverts. We can think deep thoughts, delve deep into advanced tasks, and maintain complete focus for extended periods of time, but we lose this ability completely if our neighbor's ringtone keeps going off every fifteen minutes. It seems likely that many of the old truths about leadership were first stated by extraverts. Working behind a closed door is often brought up in management training. New managers are taught to pay close attention when people close their office doors, as it's presumed to be a sign that the person in question is discouraged, depressed, or angry. I can reveal what it really means: we're simply trying to get some work done.

Introverts prefer a minimum of distracting stimuli. Our minds are pulled by a whole team of sled dogs, and we have

210

to struggle constantly to keep them all going in the same direction. They take every opportunity they can to chase after irrelevant tangents.

As I mentioned earlier, many introverts have a hard time *concentrating* around distractions. But if we don't have to concentrate, distractions aren't a problem for us. We can relax in noisy environments, and simply block the disturbances out, just like we turn passive to block out excessive stress. We can fall asleep on noisy trains, or tolerate hordes of screaming children. Extraverts, on the other hand, are activated by noises. This means that they can perform well even in the face of stress and distractions. The weakness of extraverts is their inability to relax in chaotic environments, where there are too many noises inviting them to act and react in different ways. Extraverts are usually the people who are distracted by minor background noises, like wheezing air conditioners or squeaky loudspeakers. Oddly enough, they're both sensitive and insensitive at once. A good working environment is one that caters to both personality types.

Just say no to group massages

"What does your meeting cost?" This question is written on the wall of one of IKEA's conference rooms. This is such sensible thinking that it gives me a warm fuzzy feeling. Just think of all of the meetings you've had to sit through at work. Try to estimate what percentage of these meetings you could just as well have missed. Intuitively, I'd say that eighty percent of *all* the meetings I've ever been to were a waste of my time. It's even worse when you have to travel a long way for a pointless meeting. I never cease to be amazed over the fact that we send handfuls of professionals to offices on the other side of the planet without giving them any specific tasks to perform. This happens all the time. We send a bunch of Swedish MBAs to the Tokyo office for two weeks, and instruct them to "meet some people, do some networking, and put names to faces." This 100,000-dollar investment of time and money is given the vague and immeasurable justification that it'll somehow automatically improve our collaboration.

But this is just the current zeitgeist. We live in a culture obsessed with meetings, where magic is expected to happen whenever people are brought together. Many meetings are led by outgoing jokers, who never miss an opportunity to include some bizarre exercise or other. If you object, and state that these games seem pointless to you, you'll be told that they're meant to promote collaboration. Sweaty participants are instructed to touch each other, and give group massages in a circle. This is expected to promote a sense of belonging, but if we're being honest, it's more likely to cause a Norovirus epidemic. Another popular exercise involves sitting face to face with strangers, and challenge each other to maintain eye contact without laughing. The joker in charge of the exercise pokes at you cheekily. Spontaneous reactions are forced out of people. "What do you think?", they say with a smile, and refuse to relent until they've gotten me to reveal my half-baked thoughts. At coaching classes, leaders are taught one of the most idiotic proverbs of our age: "Good feedback is always immediate, spontaneous, and sincere!" They demand to know what you think before they'll let you leave the room. These ideas were almost certainly hatched by a bunch of extraverts at some fantastic seminar where they were given unlimited access to sangria. The introverted thought process is slow, deep, and independent. It's important to understand this. *Miracle meetings* do happen, but only very rarely. A miracle meeting involves creating a situation in which *everybody* will feel at home, not just the people who naturally enjoy being seen and heard in a group context.

Special chants, corporate slogans, and mutual backslapping all seem shallow to introverts. This is why introverts often end up not taking part in group processes.

Extraverts make decisions quickly, and form opinions almost immediately. Introverts wear their poker faces while the cogs are turning behind the scenes. When the extraverts are nod to each other in agreement, the silence of the introverts is also interpreted as an expression of agreement.

Meetings, meetings, meetings

Far too many meetings involve little else than conversations about other meetings. Minutes that nobody will ever read are written, and activities are planned, only to be immediately forgotten about. On occasion, I've been summoned to compulsory informational meetings where the message was essentially that there wouldn't be any information until the next meeting. If you've spent well over an hour on a commuter train to get to this compulsory meeting, your blood might well be boiling by this point. These days, there seems to be an unwritten law that everybody has to demand ridiculous amounts of information, and want to communicate and partake of every last piece of it all the time. It seems to me that ignorance really is bliss. How about this: you do your job, and I'll do mine? I think meetings are too often just opportunities for self-promotion and jockeying for position. Introverts tend to get overlooked in this kind of context. At one place where I used to work, we had a compulsory weekly meeting. At most of these meetings, we had nothing to discuss, so our boss would blurt out things like: "So, does anybody have a good joke?" Too often, meetings seem to be ends in themselves. The US electronics chain Best Buy has dared to try a new, more liberal approach to their work. They've realized that people like to be treated like adults, even at work! As a result of this, they've adopted a number of policies that give each individual worker the freedom to decide how, when, and where their work gets done. They don't put any emphasis on how much you work; they only look at the results you get.

One of the things I like about Best Buy's strategy is that they've stopped having compulsory meetings. It's always up to you to decide if you have time to go or not. This sounds like a paradise for introverts! Google has acquired a reputation for being a great employer. For example, Google employees are allowed to spend twenty percent of their working hours on their own ideas. Rumor has it that fifty percent of Google's patents have resulted from this practice.

How long is a piece of string?

Another thing that annoys me is how long meetings can run. Every meeting is expected to be an hour long by default. As a consequence of this, they usually run *at least* that long. Studies have shown that any task generally takes as long to perform as the time available for performing it. We adjust our psychology and approach to the work so that the task will fill the time we have.

A Finnish company introduced the rule that no meeting should *ever* last longer than fifteen minutes. This allowed them to keep their meetings brief and to the point. There was none of the usual small talk, and the participants all stayed very focused. I think this is a great attitude. Perhaps the opinion that most of the time spent in corporate meetings is wasted is mostly held by introverts, but the way I see it, it's time spent doing nothing, that could have been used to create value instead.

Reluctantly inspired

In my professional life, I've learned to limit my spontaneous conversations to a few lines of polite small talk. This is the rule I stick to when I have stuff to do. Talking to extraverts can be a real time sink. Sometimes, without showing any sensitivity at all to your situation, they'll begin to give you detailed accounts of their children's graduations, their ketogenic diet, or some other irrelevant matter. The remarkable thing is that this unrequested river of speech will occasionally yield nuggets of pure gold. Even though I hate being interrupted, I have to confess that many of my best ideas have been given to me by some pretty intrusive people. There's a relationship between extraverts and introverts that can really make sparks fly from time to time. One effect I've noticed is that extraverts' moods will occasionally rub off on me in such a way that I find myself still grinning long after the conversation ended.

Tips for bosses – bringing out the best in the introverts in your teams

- ✓ Introverts perform less well in stressful or noisy conditions. This is what sets them apart from extraverts, who gear up in those situations instead. Extraverts rise to the pressure, while introverts get distracted and passive.
- ✓ Introverts want to block the noise out. We need our own rooms to be truly efficient at work. For this reason, it can be a good idea to encourage working from home. There are few places in which I can achieve the same level of focus that I can in my own study.
- ✓ Hard and focused learning is best done in solitude, according to expertise researcher Anders Ericsson. A rock-solid, introverted focus is the tool that will allow you to polish your talent until it shines.
- ✓ Multitasking is never really very efficient, because of the setup time involved in switching between different tasks. This is easy to forget when you're skipping from one task to another, and feeling energized from being activated to the max, and keeping lots of ideas going at once. But as a wise person once said: "You can be very productive

without being particularly efficient." Working in sequence is the best way for most people, but this is even more true of introverts. Encourage a culture that allows us to handle one task at a time.

✓ Advance planning is a must. We need time to prepare. One of the true strengths of introverts is our ability to absorb large amounts of impersonal information, and then sort this information inside our minds, by twisting, turning, and examining it. After this analysis, we'll often have seen something completely different than whatever appeared to be the case at first. An introvert's powers of analysis are wasted if there's no time for reflection. If you want to have decisions made then and there, at the table, you should provide a lot of the relevant materials well in advance of the meeting, so that the participating introverts can play to their strengths.

✓ Creativity is a seed that needs to germinate in solitude. Studies have shown that group brainstorming sessions tend to be dominated by their most verbal participants. The strength of your voice determines whether or not your idea will win approval. There's nothing wrong with discussing and thinking things through in groups per se, it's just that the mind of an introvert needs to mull things over in solitude. Their best ideas don't usually appear in the meeting room. They come much later, in the bathroom, behind the wheel, in bed, or on the running track.

Introversion in specialist professions

It's a freezing cold yet stunningly beautiful morning. I'm driving along under a bright sky, and the roads, still wet from the rain, glisten like gold in the sunlight. By the time I reach the entrance to the academy, I'm full of anticipation. Anne-Mette, the instructor, meets me at the door.

Her demeanor is positive, and her posture straight and proud. Her eyes are icy blue, and she has a way about her

216

that inspires trust. I'm hoping that she'll be able to help me learn what kind of personality you need to have to be able to do one of the most extremely demanding jobs around.

Once we're inside their airy building, we're joined by the friendly whirlwind Åsa. She smiles a lot, and describes herself as one hundred percent extraverted. She's specialized in the advanced and rigorous selection process that they use here. It's a standardized test system called FEAST, which measures every dimension of competence, personality, and cognition that you could imagine. Anne-Mette and Åsa provide training that's so demanding in terms of cognitive ability that only a tiny proportion of the population would make the cut. They're on the lookout for talents who have the right stuff. The job we're discussing here is that of an air-traffic controller.

I'm here to perform a field study investigating the significance of extraversion for extreme professional roles of this kind. I sit down with them, and time flies by. They share freely of their knowledge, and before I know it, it's mid-afternoon.

So what does extraversion have to do with this particular line of work?

Extraversion is a dimension of the personality that covers much more than the extent to which you enjoy being in social situations. The social aspect of extraversion is better understood as a symptom of the way that your brain processes information. Introverted and extraverted personalities process the events that occur in their environments differently. Listed on the next page are some of the factors that have been statistically shown to be strengths of introversion and extraversion.

Introverts:

- ✓ Are able to maintain their focus for extended periods of time. Don't get bored easily, and don't need as many breaks from work.
- ✓ Are good at improvising, and at managing situations that they haven't received specific training for.
- ✓ Are attentive to details and quality deviations.
- ✓ Have slow but deep thought processes. This means that introverts generally tend to have higher IQs, and to cognitively deliberate over most of their decisions.

Extraverts:

- ✓ Are good at keeping several balls in the air, i.e., work on several different projects at once.
- ✓ Take in lots of information through their sight, hearing, and other senses. Their alpha waves are stronger than those of introverts. Alpha waves are related to perceptual ability.
- ✓ Maintain their capacity well, even when stressed.
- ✓ Have fast but shallow thought processes, and form opinions about situations very quickly. They make quick decisions, and tend to base them on routine procedures. If no routine is established, they tend to succumb to affect, and base their decisions on their gut feelings.

The reason why flight-traffic controllers are such an interesting group to examine is this: most other jobs are reasonably forgiving. There's always some way to manage a professional role so that it can be successfully performed by a person who has a certain set of strengths and weaknesses. A truly introverted HR manager, for instance, could choose to specialize in salary systems and labor law, rather than the more social aspects of the job, such as interviewing. This means that in most professions, you'll find that there are successful people from all over the spectrum, even though they might seem to be the *wrong fit* for the job. Some star

218

salespeople are introverts, and some of the best coders are extraverts.

The role of a flight-traffic controller *isn't flexible* in this way. There's only one way to do this job, and that's what makes it so interesting. Critical requisites for a flight-traffic controller are the ability to take in information quickly, the ability to judge it correctly, and the ability to draw conclusions about what will happen next. Here are three important abilities that an air-traffic controller needs:

- ✓ The ability to maintain parallel trains of thought. It's absolutely essential that you be able to keep several balls in the air.
- ✓ An air-traffic controller needs to be good at collaborating with others. For example, this could be a matter of understanding what information the person on the other end needs.
- ✓ The ability to make clear, rational, and quick decisions.

The question I asked, then, was this: Are air-traffic controllers introverts or extraverts, or are both social preferences represented among them?

This meeting, which I expected to last for an hour, turned into an all-day exercise, and produced some very interesting discussions. Åsa and Anne-Mette generously shared their insights into what goes on behind the scenes while people are being trained for this profession. We tested their students, active air-traffic controllers, and instructors, who had worked as air-traffic controllers themselves in the past.

The study showed that the respondents were clustered around the middle of the spectrum. Most of the people who had passed the tests displayed a balance between introversion and extraversion.

The extraverted aspect gives them good perception, good multitasking, and the ability to make decisions quickly, while the introverted aspect is essential in that it enables them to maintain their focus during long periods of repetitive work.

People who were too extraverted would probably start looking for something else to do before long, because of how low the level of variety is. They wouldn't be sufficiently activated. Perhaps they'd be better off if they made a career move, and became instructors? This could explain why this particular group differed from the rest in that particular regard; the instructors were the most extraverted of the respondents. Perhaps another outlet for extraverts could be the cultivation of colorful and demanding activities outside of work? As it happens, many professional air-traffic controllers have very active hobbies.

People who were too introverted would probably not be good enough at multitasking, and would probably also have poor stress management, which would cause obvious problems here.

I don't think either extreme would be very well suited to this profession. Instead, the ideal mix is a successful fusion of introverted and extraverted traits.

A misconception regarding competence

Suppose that two new co-workers join your workplace one day. They're twins, and look almost exactly alike, but you soon notice that they behave very differently.

Chip is a friendly and outgoing guy, who has a natural and genuine way with people. His hearty laughter is constantly heard echoing around the hallways. He's loud, and gets away with it by being such a warm-hearted person. He even bakes muffins for the Friday coffee sometimes. He has an amusing anecdote prepared for every situation. Chip becomes very popular at the office from day one.

His brother, Dale, is quite different. Dale is reticent, restrained, and quiet. He hardly greets his co-workers in the mornings. Instead, he sits down at his desk with the door closed whenever he gets the chance. At the Friday coffee, he picks up a muffin and sneaks off to his office rather than joining in. Dale is the object of a fair bit of office gossip, and some people say he's arrogant. One day, the economy hits a slump, and the company has to lay people off. The shadow of redundancy falls on Chip and Dale. Their HR manager is told that one of them has to go. "Keep the most competent one," the CEO says, before rushing off. An hour later, Chip is uncharacteristically quiet as he packs his stuff in a banana crate. This may seem strange, but there's a fascinating psychology at work here. This is the effect of a phenomenon related to our estimations of others.

You see, we're wired in such a way that we tend to regard arrogance as a sign of competence. Characters like Dr. House on TV are good examples of this kind of prejudice. Something within us deceives us into believing that outgoing people are less competent than those who are more withdrawn. Introverts can seem arrogant and uptight. Sometimes, we don't just seem to be those things: we *are* them.

What will I be when I grow up?

A bearded gentleman by the name of John Holland has studied how introverts can make the most of their talents. According to him, there are a few general career paths that are particularly well-suited for our preference. These are the roles he believes that introverts can perform the best in:

Investigative roles: These are roles that involve a lot of thinking. Their work is characterized by frequent shifts between focusing on the details and focusing on the big picture. Their tasks involve searching for information and clues. Typical examples are advisory roles, like those performed by lawyers and psychologists.

Social roles: These are roles that are based on communication with other people. Typical examples are teachers and police officers.

Realistic roles: These roles are down-to-earth in nature. They include foresters, machine technicians, and craftspeople. Examples of people whose jobs belong to this category are electricians, carpenters, lumberjacks, and healthcare professionals like nurses and doctors.

Enterprising roles: Roles that involve defining and managing projects. These roles involve leadership, risk assessment, and mediation.

Artistic roles: Aesthetic professions that involve working with colors, shapes, and design. These jobs are characterized by free work processes. This category includes illustrators, artists, and art directors.

Conventional roles: These are clearly defined roles, which follow precisely defined routines and processes. This work is designed to destroy your soul and smother you in your sleep. The job category can be defined as "any position within a government agency".

Group dynamics – nobody is as dumb as all of us together

Gather a number of individuals, make them think of themselves as a group, and presto! You've created something that represents both the worst and the best that humanity has to offer.

A few decades ago, a study was made of how people think in groups. It was determined that a group of people is generally able to produce more ideas than any solitary genius. The expression "collective intelligence", which is sometimes rephrased as the *wisdom of the crowd*, was coined. But, as I pointed out, groups represent both the best and the worst of humanity. Which outcome you get depends on how the group is formed. Introversion and extraversion play a very special role in group dynamics. Let's begin by exploring the less positive aspects of groups.

Group weakness 1: The bystander effect

In 1964, a woman called Kitty Genovese was killed by a knife-wielding maniac. Her murder took place in an apartment building, which was full of witnesses at the time. However, nobody intervened or called the police, because everybody simply assumed that somebody else would do something. This group dynamic has been recreated in studies since then. There's a definite downside to being part of a group: the greater the number of people who witness something, the less responsibility each individual feels to intervene. Everybody trusts that the group will do something, rather than acting themselves. This is called the bystander effect, and it's the first of the negative effects of groups.

Group weakness 2: Deindividuation

When you see a rowdy crowd of sports fans on the verge of rioting, what you're seeing is a different kind of group dynamic. People turn into animals when their favorite team loses a home game. Park benches are knocked over, and dumpsters get set on fire. Stores are vandalized, and strangers are assaulted by packs of raging cavemen. This effect is called deindividuation. What it means is that the larger a group gets, the less its members will act as individuals. As we all know, it's never a lone hooligan that goes berserk, it's always a crowd. When the group grows large enough, the ego gets taken out of the equation, and the sense of personal responsibility goes with it.

Group weakness 3: Peer pressure

Did anybody ever take up smoking for any other reason than peer pressure? Peer pressure is an incredibly powerful effect, which can even make us doubt our own senses.

Group weakness 4: Groupthink

Bringing a sufficient number of men with huge egos and huge beards together in a group can produce a phenomenon known as groupthink. This is characterized by hubris, as the group begins to imagine that they know better than the rest of the world. A group that's under the influence of groupthink has no doubts at all regarding its own expertise. The history of our world is like a daisy chain of events caused by groupthink. The Chernobyl disaster is considered to be one of them. Outside experts warned the management at the power plant not to raise the reactors' output, but the management team felt that they knew better than everybody else. The rest, as they say, is history. The number one cause of groupthink is that the members of a group are too similar to one another. When they're all the same age, and went to the same schools, and live in the same place, there's a great risk that the culture they establish will be based on mutual backslapping.

Group weakness 5: The winner's curse

In competitive situations, active personalities can reveal some pretty mean streaks. Extraverts tend to get energized, inspired, and performance-oriented in any context that's even remotely competitive. In situations oriented towards performance and competition, extraverts often see red. The larger the number of competitors, the greater the risk you'll run of suffering what's known as the winner's curse. Let's take an auction as an example. If you have two people bidding against you, you might go as far as bidding 1,200 dollars in the heat of the bidding war. But when the number of competitors increases, our ability to make decisions is impaired. If you were competing with ten other people instead, it's quite likely that you would have ended up bidding more than 1,200. The adrenalin and excitement would cause you to pay more than it was actually worth to you, just to get the win. This effect of group activity is called the winner's curse, because the person who wins often ends up paying a price that's too high.

Introversion vs. groupthink

In the previous section, we went over five negative aspects of group behavior. But how are they related to introversion?

One of the strengths possessed by introverts is that they can mitigate groupthink by thinking and acting as individuals. Studies have shown that the recurring feature of introverts is keeping their distance to groups. We don't feel that we belong to groups to the same extent that extraverts do. They value membership in groups based on the value that others assign to it. Introverts put greater emphasis on their own estimation of the group.

There's a cost attached to having opinions that conflict with those of your group, and the currency used to pay it is social acceptance. The exchange rate of this currency seems higher to an extraverted person, who lives to be around other people. Introverts don't expect somebody else to call the police. We don't feel our egos dissolve in groups. Our decision processes depend on our having long periods of time available to reflect and peel away our emotions. We often hold opinions that make other people uncomfortable, and we don't have a problem with expressing them. All of this makes the introverted personality the natural antidote to some of the issues caused by group dynamics. Thinking outside of the box is characteristic of introverts. After all, thinking inside the box generally means that you're thinking the same things as everybody else in the group. A group psychology expert once described the ultimate group like this: *Its members have independent personalities, and contribute unique information.*

It's obvious that many of the greatest and most radical reforms in history have resulted from positive group dynamics. The Arab Spring, the March on Washington, and the fall of the Berlin wall all depended on this positive aspect of group behavior.

Well-documented experiments have been carried out to investigate how to create efficient groups. It may be something of a cliché, but the fact is that the recipe for a successful group has just a single ingredient: *diversity*. Diversity will give you people with different points of view, thanks to their different backgrounds, values, skill sets, and beliefs. For this reason, you should try to ensure that your group includes introverts as well as extraverts, men as well as women, people from different generations, and anything else that will guarantee the group's diversity. The fact that everybody is smarter than somebody else is true, but only in diverse groups.

Research is underway

This topic has obviously been the object of an impressive amount of research. Despite this, introversion remains something of a mystery, that's still being explored. We do know, on a purely hormonal level, that the more introverted you are, the lower your tolerance for the neurotransmitter dopamine is likely to be.

Lots of studies are still being performed on this topic, and psychologists haven't quite managed to agree on a correct definition of the concept. If you'd like a very brief summary of the main points on which they've actually reached consensus, the following three characteristics are the most obvious cases.

1. *Independence.* We have a weaker social need than extraverts. We're not particularly influenced by groupthink, and we stand by our opinions even in heated debates.
2. *Focus.* We're able to keep working on a task for a long time, and maintain full focus throughout without tiring. The reason for this is thought to be our low tolerance for dopamine; which means that we pretty much always think that there's enough going on around us. This is why introverts don't need as much variety as extraverts do.
3. *Reflection.* Our thought process is broad, thorough, and deep. Our decisions are the results of careful deliberation, as opposed to spontaneous.

Everything comes down to the nature of our minds, which process large amounts of information even in the absence of external stimuli. A psychologist expressed it this way: *Extraverts chatter on the outside, and introverts chatter on the inside.*

The reason for introverts' tendency to feel overloaded by social interactions has yet to be determined. Studies of brain activity have indicated that introverts process more information at any given moment, and that this may contribute to their getting exhausted sooner. I find this idea quite flattering, but it's not yet been established that this is really the case. Another riddle is why people have these different preferences at all. One theory that's been offered takes an evolutionary perspective. It's been shown that people who have lived on islands for a few generations tend to be more introverted than people who migrate to the same islands. This preference seems to exemplify a certain dynamic: extraverts move on, and establish new settlements and cities, while introverts tend to stay behind and develop existing settlements. Of course, this is a very rough generalization.

Am I *more* than just an introvert?

People are complicated, and of course there's more to them than just their social preferences. An introvert isn't just a shy type who can solve tricky problems. Biology isn't the whole story; the society we grow up in has a great influence on us, too. We're shaped by the teenage culture we enter, and the accepted values that we're taught. When it comes to the psychology of personality, extraversion/introversion is one of five characteristics that are supposedly shared by all people on this planet. These are collectively referred to as the *Big Five personality traits*. The other four traits are the following:

Conscientiousness. This is a measure of your self-discipline, attention to detail, and structured behavior. You could quite reasonably claim that this trait reflects a person's level of ambition. Possessing this trait to a great degree is commonly referred to as having "good character".

Openness to experience. This trait has to do with curiosity and thirst for knowledge. Your openness regulates things like your willingness to seek out new impressions, and your awareness of your own emotional life and the emotional lives of others.

Neuroticism. This reflects how you manage your negative emotions. A very neurotic person has a lot of anger, anxiety, and instability within herself.

Agreeableness. This is a measure of your disposition to cooperate with others. A high level of this is characterized by optimism and good social skills. You possess empathy, and tend to help other people. A low level indicates a competitive attitude to other people, and suspicion of strangers.

Research has shown that introversion is independently connected to some of the other Big Five traits. *Conscientiousness* is positively correlated with introversion. The more introverted you are, the better you'll tend to be at getting your work done.

Unfortunately, there's also a correlation between neuroticism and introversion. The more introverted you are, the more likely you are to have an above-average degree of *neuroticism*. This means that you'll tend to be more suspicious of people, and less positive about life in general, than extraverts are. I prefer to think of it as introverts being less naive, and more realistic in their outlook.

To climb or not to climb

I was taking a management class, which had mainly involved fairly peaceful exercises and discussions so far. A curtain was raised, and the huge room was immediately filled with nervous murmurs. A climbing wall towered over us. Many of the participants were so eager for competition that they were bouncing up and down in place, as this exercise was obviously going to involve some kind of competition. My body went limp. I looked out over the crowd, and saw a number of lowered faces: people like me. I should add at this point that I've always been afraid of heights. The reactions within the group were fairly stereotypical, as far as I could tell. Under pressure, extraverts take action, and introverts become passive. What happened next would give me one of the most important lessons I've learned in recent years. The coach cunningly walked up to the wall, pointed at a grip he could almost reach from the floor, and said: "Your goal is to reach this grip." I felt my pulse drop like a rock. This seemed like a very easy task. I went from a state of stress to calm within a number of seconds. He continued: "There's also a bonus target – reaching the top." The effect this had on the group was very interesting. The competitive-minded extraverts all set their sights on the bonus target right away, and they all made it all the way up. The introverted participants, including myself, took on the main goal. As it was so easy to reach, I tried to go a little higher, just to see how far I would make it. *All* of the participants made it to the top! I'm convinced that this would never have happened if that had been the main goal. The threshold was low enough to get everybody onto the wall to try it out. This gave me a lot of food for thought, and influenced my approach to all of the leadership roles I've had. I think that establishing an easy main target and a more challenging bonus target is key for activating both extraverts and introverts.

Summary for extraverts

- ✓ Introverts are thoughtful and independent. This often puts us at odds with the prevailing values in our societies. This is positive in the sense that it counteracts groupthink. Groupthink is what happens when a group ceases to be critical of its own behavior.
- ✓ Introverts like to plan and structure their work in peace. This makes them very independent workers. Introverts don't always feel that working in groups is a good way to get results.
- ✓ Introverts are more sensitive to noisy and messy working environments than extraverts are. This means that most introverts get distracted in open plan offices.

Finding Your Cork Tree

"There's about ten of us; we meet once or twice a month to cook gourmet food, drink fine wines, and socialize. Many of the people who come are pretty influential in the business world, so it's a good opportunity to network. Would you like to tag along?"

I open my mouth, and then close it again, resisting my initial impulse. I came close to agreeing to go out of gratitude, without thinking. But then I remembered that that's just not my kind of party. I don't enjoy playing games of social one-upmanship with superficial acquaintances. I'm no good at strategic networking, and trying to connect with people to further my career. If I don't like somebody, it wouldn't make any difference if this person was the CEO of Google. But naturally, I'm flattered to be invited. I think we often accept invitations just to be polite. However, it's important for your personal growth that you answer invitations based on your natural preference. You shouldn't make extraverted decisions just because you live in such an extraverted world. Find your way back to your cork tree! The way I see it, making active choices of this kind means that you're taking part in an awakening. This introverted movement, which has only just begun to stir, isn't about shouting or slamming doors, or manning barricades and burning your underwear. It's simply about choosing not to do things that don't suit our *true* personalities. I've admitted to myself that I'd rather read Batman comics in sweatpants than eat a gourmet dinner in a suit. The "friendly takeover" that's mentioned in the title of this book is, more than anything, about beginning to view introverted traits as desirable. It's time we learned to appreciate thoughtfulness, independence, and deep focus. I long for a future where searching for "introvert" won't give me lots of hits about serial killers, and where recruitment ads don't all state that the person they're looking is *outgoing*.

At the close of the 1980s, Madonna had a huge hit with her song "Express yourself", and it seems that the world really took her message to heart. Today, everything seems to revolve around expressing yourself.

Texting, email, tweets, status updates, and phone calls are a dime a dozen (often even less!). The flow of communication has turned into a tidal wave that's carrying our entire society along with it. It can seem that being the odd one out, who hates phone calls and meetings with a passion, would be a bad thing. But there's also comfort to be found in reminding yourself that introverts, despite these phobias, are the dominant personality type in the worlds of academia, technology, and aesthetics.

The most important part of coming out as an introvert has nothing to do with how others ought to be relating to you; it's all about how you relate to yourself.

Introvert Carina says: "As I grow older and wiser, I find myself becoming more and more comfortable with my nature. There's a difference in how I relate to myself, and an even greater difference in how I relate to others. I don't feel out of place as often, and I don't try to change my behavior; I think of how to use my preference in the best possible way instead. I also allow my children to be the way they are: a little introverted, calm, and secure."

People who are mistaken about their own preference are referred to as pseudoverts. Sometimes, this happens because the influence of the environment in which they grew up is so strong that they've lost touch with their true preferences. Sometimes, it's because they stubbornly *want* to be extraverts, and filter out anything that indicates that the opposite might be the case. I'd like to be able to help others identify and accept their natural preferences. Once you've accepted your preference, skipping things that don't feel right for you, and turning down an invitation now and then, will become much easier to do.

Introvert Carina says: "The danger of turning invitations down to spend time alone under your cork tree is that if you do it too often, the invitations might eventually stop coming. And that *would* be a shame. It's all about finding a balance, and making sure that you don't let your relief show too plainly when a social event that you weren't looking forward to is canceled."

I found a short quote somewhere in the icy wastes of the Internet. It's a useful mantra for introverts, which I often repeat out loud to myself. It goes like this:

"I'm not angry, depressed, or asocial. I just don't feel like talking to anybody for a while, and that's OK."

Sacrifice

A few weeks ago, Hanna and I went to a release party. The band that a close friend of ours is in was releasing an album. We squeezed into a tiny club full of drunken Danes. Hanna and I were standing up front, by the stage, with some friends of ours. We soon found ourselves competing for space with a bunch of middle-aged men who were revisiting the bliss of their teenage years. It took me an hour or so to run out of social steam, and after that I pressed up against the wall and glued my eyes to my phone. I was out of my element at this event, and I'd known that I would be before we came. Going anyway was a conscious choice on my behalf. My friend was very happy that we showed up.

Compromising your own needs to show support for other people is a loving gesture. There are many things of value to be achieved outside of our comfort zones. Some people would even claim that everything of value lies beyond your comfort zone, but I realize that, as a rule, the people who say this are extraverted job coaches. However, the fact remains that compromises strengthen relationships.

Introversion – from a diagnosis to a strength

The most complicated step can be figuring out what your preference actually is. We often have a hard time defining it even to ourselves, because of how our biological programming is mixed up with the norms that regulate our behavior. There's also often an unclear measure of *who we want to be* involved. Some people are excited by the idea of being a dominant verbal entrepreneur. If these people take a self-assessment test, they're prone to fudge their responses a little to reinforce this self-image. Many people I speak to identify with both introverted and extraverted needs. In many situations, we truly are both. If you put 200 people in a room and ask them questions, you'll perceive them as a very introverted group. Everybody falls silent once the group they're in grows large enough. If you take an introverted group of people, and ask them to argue in favor of something they care passionately about, you'll see a fire in them that isn't usually associated with introversion. My point here is that we all behave differently in different situations. Our behavior is influenced by the environment we're in. In this media-conscious age, there are many eccentrics such as myself who have learned to present themselves as extraverted in social situations. For this reason, determining people's preference based on their appearance or clothes is no longer possible. Introverts don't all dress like Carlton or Steve Urkel anymore. The best way to figure your own preference out is to think of *what you do when you're free to do anything you want*. Therein lies the answer.

Clams make beautiful pearls

It's often said that actions speak louder than words. This is no longer the case. Even a brilliant idea is dead in the water if it's sold in a mediocre way. Ingenious products have had to give way to products marketed by quicker tongues, with better sales pitches. In this extraverted age, a strong voice will always trump quality and execution.

I'd like to describe a behavior that I've often observed in introverts. We like to wrap ourselves up in a warm blanket of our own thoughts. We sit in our rooms and write, draw, analyze, sing, code, or whatever it is we do. We invest an enormous focus and oceans of time into chiseling things out with our brains. The problem comes next: for many of us, this is the end of our efforts. We settle. We sit there with these products of our thoughts, waiting for somebody to *discover* us. We think that it's up to somebody else, usually our boss, to boost us and promote our efforts. I'd like to advise all introverts out there to learn the art of marketing themselves, even if self-promotion makes them uncomfortable. Put the things you produce out there, in the real world. Network with people who can help you achieve your goals, even if it makes your social muscles ache. Make a connection, and direct your energy outwards, at the world. It's much easier to find an audience today than it was just ten years ago. Thanks to social media, you can put your art out there without ever having to speak to a single sleazy gallerist.

My conclusion is that introverts tend to overproduce and undersell. For some reason, we don't have a problem with spending 600 hours writing a book, but we can find it almost impossible to spend thirty minutes on actually reading a publishing deal.

Some people keep great works of art hidden away in lonely galleries. There are plenty of Helen Kellers out there, with drawers full of incredible stories that nobody has read. I know of young people who have created spectacular pieces of software, but who don't have the energy to try to make any money off of it. Introversion is a gift that makes you destined for more than being a dreamer. Use this gift to maximize the results you want to achieve in the world. I used to be that person, with a drawer full of novels. Then, I decided to get in touch with some publishers, and that's how my own career path began.

So they had to take Ferdinand home...

In the end, I found my way home as an introvert. People pay me to write books, and to lecture on topics that I'm already passionate about. When I lecture, I get to do it without suffering any distractions or interruptions.

I spend many of my days in an oasis of my own design. My office is full of books on philosophy, psychology, and other subjects that I love. When I close the door to it, the outside world ceases to exist. The walls are decorated with inspiring pictures of all kinds of things, from amazing architecture to creative photographic experiments. I fill the room with music that I can immerse myself in, and wear my most comfortable clothes. There's nothing but me, my writing, and my imagination in the room. I own my calendar, because I'm my own boss. There's a contradiction here: I feel free, even though I work harder than ever now that I'm fully the slave of my own ambition. This existence suits me extremely well, because now my batteries are always charged and ready for a meeting. When I go to visit the man village, to see somebody, I genuinely enjoy spending time with them. Today, I get to do the things that truly interest me, which is the greatest luxury I can imagine. Instead of adapting myself to an extraverted world, I turned inward, and found a role that suits me as I am. Regardless of where my career ends up taking me, I've found my core self, and I'll be able to monitor and affirm it going forward. I know what I am.

Our callings in life vary wildly, even among introverts. People can find meaning in writing code, forestry, running a second-hand bookstore, or swimming across Lake Michigan in a renaissance costume. It doesn't matter what your calling is, as long as you find it.

A philosopher once said that the meaning of life is to stay in motion, and to keep trying different things until you eventually find the thing that you're meant to do.

I'm doing what I was meant to do, and that gives me a deep sense of inner satisfaction. The point is that you should do something that you find rewarding in itself, instead of trading your time away for money. Now, I'm sitting here still, under my favorite cork tree, smelling the espresso, just quietly. I'm very happy. Just like Ferdinand.

In closing, I'd like to tell you about a conversation I had in a chat with an acquaintance of mine. She explained that she'd been upset by something her friends had said to her. They had called her selfish, and an introvert. I explained to her that "introvert" isn't an insult, and told her about the advantages of being an introvert. I'd like to give all of you the same advice that I gave her:

If somebody calls you an introvert, just say "Thanks."

Test – Are you Stuck in a Closet?

In this test, you'll be presented with a series of pairs of statements. For each pair, please choose the option, A or B, that you feel describes you the best. Don't choose the answer that reflects *who you want to be*, pick the answer that reflects who you actually are. One of the most common sources of error in personality tests is that we tend to respond based on who we wish we were. Don't fall into that trap. Be honest with yourself! There will be instructions for adding up your score at the end of the test. Your score will give you an estimate of where you are on the scale from extravert to introvert.

1

A. Social events sometimes overwhelm you. You can feel completely exhausted afterwards.

B. Meeting new people inspires you and feeds you energy. Social events can energize you.

2

A. Entering a room full of people you don't know makes you feel uncomfortable.

B. Entering a room full of people you don't know makes you feel excited

3

A. After a week of business meetings, and working closely with colleagues, you'd like nothing better than to relax on your own, or with your closest family.

B. After a week of hard work in close collaboration with colleagues, you'd like nothing more than to call some friends and get a party going somewhere.

4

A. You work best in sequence. You need to concentrate on one task at a time, and finish what you're doing before moving on to the next thing.

B. You don't mind working on parallel activities, and can switch back and forth between them without any problems. The variety gives you momentum, and feeds you energy that helps you perform better.

5

A. You avoid discussing things with people you don't know. In the supermarket, or at the post office, you exchange pleasantries, but nothing more.

B. You seek eye contact and social exchanges. You're often the one to initiate a conversation when you're with strangers.

6

A. Your speech is characterized by pauses and thoughtfulness. When somebody asks you a question, you like to hold on giving an answer until you've had the time to choose the right words.

B. You don't think too much about what you're going to say, and your words are generally the same as your thoughts.

7

A. You're bad at small talk, and trying to indulge in it makes you feel affected and fake. You don't initiate interactions with people you don't already know.

B. You're quick to speak, and have an easy time speaking about almost anything with almost anybody. That's why you have such an easy time connecting with strangers.

8

A. When the phone rings, you'll often let it go to the answer machine. You prefer calling back later, when it suits you.

B. You let go of anything you're doing when the phone rings, and answer it right away. Most things can wait until your phone call is finished.

9

A. You minimize your phone time. This means that most of your calls are short, and that you tend to have a specific reason for calling.

B. When you're bored, you'll often pick up your phone and call a friend for no particular reason.

10

A. You don't mind staying in the background. You make little effort to draw attention to yourself. You find being in the spotlight uncomfortable.

B. You're often the life of the party. It's not even really a role you seek actively, it's just what happens. But you enjoy being close to the center of events.

11

A. Your concentration is sensitive to disturbances, such as loud noises, or other people's conversations or messy desks.

B. Your concentration isn't particularly sensitive to disturbances, such as loud noises, or other people's conversations or messes.

12

A. You often feel that the topic under discussion is quite trite. Talking about it just seems like a waste of words.

B. Superficial conversations are good conversations, too. To you, they're just another way of getting closer to the person you're speaking to.

13

A. At parties, you tend to get stuck in conversations with one or a few people, rather than spending a little time talking with each person.

B. You often initiate conversations at parties, and speak to lots of different people.

14

A. You often feel uncomfortable and smothered around people. Larger social situations are especially draining.

B. You feel relaxed and comfortable among people. Even being in large social situations doesn't take any effort for you.

15

A. You tend to keep your emotions on the inside, rather than displaying them openly. At times, you feel like you're wearing a mask, or poker face.

B. You leak emotions. This can make it difficult for you to conceal your feelings about the people around you. They can tell how you feel about them, whether you want them to know or not.

16

A. You don't get bored easily, and you can find peaceful activities stimulating.

B. You need variation to feel activated. You get bored easily.

17

A. Your ability to perform intellectually suffers negligible effects after a night of very little sleep.

B. Your ability to perform intellectually suffers greatly after a night of very little sleep.

18

   A. You have a hard time approaching people you don't know.

   B. You have an easy time making new friends, and you find something to like in most people.

19

   A. When strangers join the group, you become more quiet than you would normally be.

   B. When strangers join the group, you'll often raise your voice to get heard and win people's attention.

20

   A. You have a pretty small number of friends, to whom you have deep ties.

   B. Your social network includes a large number of acquaintances, and you like it that way, although many of these relationships are pretty superficial.

21

   A. You often get the feeling that you're playing a role among people, a role that's very different from the way you act when you're alone.

   B. You're yourself all the time, for better and for worse.

22

   A. You often feel like you're being pressured and persuaded to do different things by people.

   B. You try to influence people and convince them to do what you want them to. You hold great sway over the people around you.

23

   A. You feel that you don't have very much to say.

   B. You have an easy time talking, and you reckon that you have a knack for striking up conversations with people.

24

A. In stores, you get uncomfortable when sales clerks approach you to ask what they can do for you.

B. You appreciate it when perky sales clerks approach you in stores.

25

A. You prefer the preparty to the actual night out.

B. You look forward to a night on the town, because that's where the action is.

26

A. New acquaintances and superficial contexts like cocktail parties make you break out in a cold sweat.

B. Cocktail parties with lots of new people are like social buffets to you.

27

A. You've had your best ideas while thinking things over in solitude.

B. Your best ideas were created in collaboration with others in groups.

28

A. Most meetings at a workplace serve no real purpose. There seem to be lot of people who labor under the illusion that meetings are ends in themselves.

B. You enjoy going to lots of meetings. Communication is essential. Meetings fuel innovation.

29

A. Stress causes your brain to shut down. It makes you passive and reflective, rather than inspiring you to take action.

B. Stress activates you, and raises your pulse. You respond quickly, with energy.

30

A. You like to get prepared and structure your thoughts before a meeting.

B. You're happy to improvise, and let the meeting take shape while it's underway.

31

A. You often ponder existential questions, like: "How big is the universe?"

B. You often ponder mundane questions, like: "How big does my ass look in these pants?"

32

A. If you're sitting behind a closed office door, it's for practical reasons, like a need to concentrate.

B. If you're sitting behind a closed office door, it's because you're having a bad day.

33

A. You prefer to work alone on most tasks, at least in the initial stages.

B. You enjoy working in a group, and you think of it as a natural way to achieve results.

34

A. Sudden changes of travel plans or weekly agendas are a source of stress for you. This isn't for any practical reason, it's just because it disturbs your patterns.

B. Sudden changes of travel plans or weekly agendas are exciting. Unexpected turns of events lead to adventure, new acquaintances, and interesting places.

35

A. Enjoyable company is loosely structured. You prefer to do things with other people, but without a constant emphasis on dialog. Reading a book while your partner watches TV next to you is your idea of ideal social interaction.

B. You like to get involved in intense discussions with lots of emotions, nerve, and humor. Discussions involving a lot of leeway and eye contact are your kind of thing.

36

A. You don't put much thought into your appearance. Your clothes and your appearance aren't designed to catch people's eye.

B. You've created yourself an image and an appearance that attracts a lot of attention. Bright colors, tattoos, piercings, bold outfits, and original haircuts are all useful weapons to have in your attention-grabbing arsenal.

37

A. Your default attitude to strangers is one of suspicion.

B. You think the best of anybody you don't yet know.

38

A. You have a cautious attitude to life. You think it's simply prudent not to count your chickens before they hatch, and to always plan for the worst.

B. Your default attitude to life is positive. You believe that most things will work out, as long as you maintain faith in your ability.

39

A. You focus deeply on one thing at a time. If you're in a conversation with somebody, you block out everything else that's happening around you.

B. You're present in the room, and you take in a broad array of different impressions. While you're talking, you also keep tabs on everything else that's going on around you.

40

A. You rarely permit yourself to give spontaneous answers. You want to weigh your words before you utter them. For this reason, you often begin your responses with a pause.

B. When somebody speaks to you, you tend to answer them quickly and impulsively.

41

A. You tend to try to slow other people down when it comes to activities and change. This is because you try to think ahead by a few steps. You can see that small mistakes early on could have big consequences later on in the project.

B. You feel that you're often the person to encourage others to take part in activities, or make the case for change. Most things can be solved along the way. It's much better to take action than to overthink everything.

42

A. It bothers you when people interrupt you in mid-sentence. You hate repeating yourself, and will often fall silent instead.

B. In conversations, you often get fired up, and you tend to interrupt others. You don't find being interrupted annoying, you just think of it as a natural aspect of any dialog.

43

   A. Your idea of good activities to do on your vacation is basically no activities at all.

   B. You prefer to take a vacation that includes a lot of exciting social activities.

44

   A. Spontaneous and unannounced visits from friends are usually a discomfort to you. You prefer to plan visits in advance.

   B. Unexpected visits add some fun to everyday life. You can always spare the time to talk to a friend.

45

   A. You give very little consideration to what's popular with other people in your choice of clothes, music, or literature.

   B. You care about following the fashions, trends, and values that are popular with various groups in society.

46

   A. When people around you become interested in something, such as a popular book or a successful movie, you tend to lose interest in it to some degree.

   B. When others are interested in something, it awakens your own curiosity. You want to understand what it is that they find attractive about it. Sharing this experience with them gives you a sense of connectedness.

47

   A. Your inspiration tends to come to you when you're alone with your thoughts.

   B. When you need inspiration, you turn to other people to get it.

48

   A. People tend to find you quite difficult to understand.

   B. Others find you easy to get to know.

49

A. You don't hesitate to voice an opinion that the people around you aren't comfortable with. You speak from the heart, and you think of yourself as somebody who tells the truth.

B. Your opinions impact your popularity and status. For this reason, you allow the people around you to influence your opinions.

50

A. You're quite restrictive about what you reveal about yourself.

B. When you speak to others, you tend to reveal more personal information than you intended to.

51

A. You're analytical and meticulous in your decision making. You think first, and act later.

B. You don't analyze your options very carefully; you tend to follow your intuition instead. You act first, and analyze later.

52

A. You're usually the person doing the most listening in a conversation.

B. In most conversations, you speak more than you listen.

53

A. You find speaking in front of large groups uncomfortable and unpleasant.

B. You have no problem with giving an impromptu presentation in front of a group of people.

54

A. Goals that are difficult to achieve stress you out in a way that impairs your performance.

B. Goals that are difficult to achieve spur you on in a way that boosts your performance.

55

    A. You feel that you perform the best in the mornings.

    B. You feel that you perform the best in the afternoons.

56

    A. When you feel unhappy, you close yourself off, and communicate even less with the outside world.

    B. When you feel unhappy, you act out, and share your emotions with the outside world.

57

    A. You prefer studying up on new tasks before taking them on.

    B. You learn best by doing. This makes you quick to try out new activities.

Your Test Results

Now, you've considered fifty-seven aspects of introversion and extraversion. In order to determine where you belong on the scale, you'll need to add up the number of As (introverted points) and the number of Bs (extraverted points) that you chose during the test. After this, determine your preference by subtracting B from A. This will give you a score of +57 to -57.

Results

-57 to -42 – very strongly extraverted

You're obviously somebody who possesses a lot of energy, and who likes to invest this energy in the people around you. You seek a central role in most contexts, and you're good at influencing people. Your circle of friends is probably quite large, and you have feelers out in every part of your social network. You're suited to very particular roles that involve a lot of personal communication, variation, and sudden changes. You're likely to be very alert and observant, but you're also prone to feeling understimulated.

-41 to -6 – predominantly extraverted

Even though you're essentially a socially oriented person, you have some traits from the introverted side. You're very flexible in your professional life, but you'd probably flourish the most in a professional role that allows you to do most of your work in social situations. In groups, your socially balanced nature makes you a true asset.

-5 to +5 – ambivert

You straddle the line between these two preferences. The unique thing about you is that you're energized by both social interactions and alone time. You're comfortable with working in groups, but you also enjoy exploring and processing things further on your own. People with ambiverted personalities get the best of both worlds, and are likely to succeed in many different professional roles.

+6 to -+41 – predominantly introverted

You have no difficulty carrying yourself in social situations, but you have an undeniable need for alone time if you're to feel content. You're happy to handle administrative, artistic, or quality-oriented tasks. You work well in groups, as well as in solitude.

+42 to -+57 – very strongly introverted

You're an unusually independent person, with a great degree of integrity. You're focused and stimulated, even when you're alone for extended periods of time. You're likely to have a knack for solving complicated mental challenges, and a tendency to be consumed by the tasks you're performing. You're sensitive to sudden changes, and you need to work in sequence, and have sufficient time to plan your work. You have a rich inner life, which is always vying for your attention. You visualize advanced concepts, and are good at refining ideas on your own. This talent makes you very much at home in highly specialized professional roles that demand extreme focus, creativity, and in-depth thinking.

The Cocktail Version –
Extraversion vs. Introversion

Introverts tend to:

- ✓ Seek stillness and relaxation.
- ✓ Like to work independently. Are able to work without any other people's involvement for extended periods of time, without longing for company.
- ✓ Notice details, and have a good eye for quality.
- ✓ Reflect a lot. Have good analytical powers, and make their decisions based on a number of different factors, maintaining their intellectual distance in doing so. Strive to separate emotions from logic.
- ✓ Be super focused. Often get caught up in a task for extended periods of time, without needing to take any breaks.
- ✓ Prefer to work in sequence, and perform one clearly delimited task at a time.
- ✓ Enjoy good brain function even on little sleep.
- ✓ Perform the best in the mornings.
- ✓ Be patient. Don't get bored when they're alone, and can wait for something to happen for a long time.
- ✓ Enjoy their own company. Have little need for social interaction.
- ✓ Have an easy time visualizing words. Think in images.
- ✓ Have good long-term memory.
- ✓ Listen well. In conversation, they're observant both of what's being said and what's actually being expressed.
- ✓ Prefer to think before they speak. Don't have any problems keeping a secret.
- ✓ Be independent. Aren't influenced by trends and groupthink to the same extent as extraverts. Don't feel a strong sense of belonging towards groups.
- ✓ Be sensitive to stress. Need to block the world out to be able to concentrate.
- ✓ Perform less well under pressure.

Extraverts tend to:

✓ Look for activity and adventure.

✓ React quickly. Have very active attitudes to the world. Find words and thoughts quickly.

✓ Be attentive. Are very present in the room. Are alert to their sensory impressions.

✓ Be oriented towards social interactions and relationships. Can make friends in most situations.

✓ Be optimists. Emphasize the positives in most situations. Think the best of other people, and have a lot of faith in their own abilities.

✓ Have good verbal skills. Are able to speak about most things with most people in a spontaneous and natural way. Find things that they have in common with the people around them.

✓ Be group-oriented. Blend in well with most groups.

✓ Involve other people in their activities. Gladly help others, and gladly receive the help of others.

✓ Put a lot of effort into their appearance, such as choices of clothes and haircuts. Studies have shown that extraverts prefer bright colors.

✓ Have a knack for influencing the people around them.

✓ Perform well under stress. Extraverts tend to work quicker when they're experiencing stress, without any detrimental effects to the quality of their work. Aren't particularly sensitive to disturbing noises.

✓ Feel at home in large crowds. Can be energized by situations that involve a lot of people.

✓ Enjoy receiving attention, and standing out from the crowd. For this reason, their appearance is often quite eye-catching. They don't mind being seen and heard, or being in the spotlight.

✓ Get restless when they're alone. Need to be activated by external events.

✓ Make decisions quickly. Usually know how they feel about something right away.

✓ Be able to shift back and forth between several simultaneous tasks, without getting stressed.

Sources

I like to read without being interrupted, sidetracked, or distracted. This is why I haven't referenced the name of some German man with a beard after every third sentence, and gathered all of my sources here instead. What follows is a list of relevant sources that I've used in writing this book.

Note: Is it *extrovert* or *extravert*? It's actually *extravert*, if you want to stick to correct Latin. *Extrovert* is a very old spelling error that's been around since the 1920s (it's widespread enough by now that you can get away with using either form of the word).

Note: What is the *Big Five*? This concept is mentioned in several places in the bibliography. Big Five (which is also known as the *Five Factor Model*) describes five dimensions of the personality which have proven to be present in all known human cultures. These are five traits that remain very much the same across different cultures and ages (there are also thirty underlying facets). The traits included in the Big Five are mainly thought to be biological and hereditary in nature (i.e., cases of nature rather than nurture). One of these traits is the extraversion dimension.

"Personality Trait Structure as a Human Universal"
McCrae, Robert R.; Costa Jr., Paul T.
American Psychologist, Vol 52(5), May 1997, 509-516.

The Big Five model as a whole is made up of a vast cluster of different studies.

Revised NEO Personality Inventory (NEO-PI-R) and NEO Five-Factor Inventory (NEO-FFI) manual.
Odessa, FL: Psychological Assessment Resources.
Costa, P.T., Jr. & McCrae, R.R. (1992).

Bibliography:

1. Dopamine. Introverted and extraverted traits arise because of differences in dopamine tolerance.
"Neurobiology of the Structure of Personality: Dopamine, Facilitation of Incentive Motivation, and Extraversion"
Behavioral and Brain Sciences
Richard A. Depue and Paul F. Collins (1999).

1a. Genetic component. A Russian study from 2007 looked for connections between a specific gene (DRD4) and certain variants of an enzyme (COMT). This connection has been found to influence dopamine uptake. In the study, this gene was shown to be present in test subjects who had extraverted and thrill-seeking, impulsive personality traits.
Relationship Between Dopamine System Genes and Extraversion and Novelty Seeking
V. E. Golimbet, M. V. Alfimova, I. K. Gritsenko, R. P. Ebstein (2007)

2. Sensitivity to stimuli. Introverted people react more strongly to stimuli. The source below is Hans Eysenck's famous lemon juice test. In the test, it turned out that introverts produce more saliva in response to stimuli (lemon juice, in this case).
Salivary Response to Lemon Juice as a Measure of Introversion
SBG Eysenck, HJ Eysenck - Perceptual and motor skills, (1967)

2a. More lemon juice. A later study recreated the lemon juice test with children as test subjects. (In the '70s, it seems to have been every scientist's God-given right to have a bunch of kids available for use as test subjects whenever they needed to validate some vague idea or other).
Salivary Response to Lemon Juice as a Measure of Introversion in Children

John Casey and Donald l. Mcmanis, (1971)

2b. Sensitivity to stimuli. The lemon juice test has been performed several times. This is another study where it was used. It's a good thing that the topic of introversion isn't limited to issues related to salivation.

"The Relation Between Introversion and Salivation"
Corcoran, D. W. J. (1964)
The American Journal of Psychology, Vol 77(2), 298-300.

2c. Tolerance for noise. In a study, introverts and extraverts were allowed to choose the volume at which a sound was played back while they performed a concentration exercise. Extraverts consistently selected a louder volume.

"Preferred Stimulation Levels in Introverts and Extroverts: Effects on Arousal and Performance"
Geen, Russell G. (1984)
Journal of Personality and Social Psychology, Vol 46(6), Jun 1984, 1303-1312.

2d. White noise. A comparison was made of the effects of white noise on groups of introverted and extraverted children. The extraverts were more resistant as a result of their higher tolerance for dopamine.

Noise Tolerance and Extraversion in Children
Colin d. Elliott (1971)

2e. Degree of activation. A study was performed in 1983, to investigate Eysenck's hypothesis regarding the lower dopamine tolerance of introverts. Groups of test subjects including introverted and extraverted individuals were manipulated using caffeine. The effects in terms of activation were measured. The conclusion was that the introverts in the test groups had an easier time reaching a higher degree of activation than the extraverts.

Extraversion and Electrodermal Activity: Arousability and the Inverted-U
Barry D. Smith (1983)

2f. Pain threshold. In one of Hans Eysenck's legendary experiments, differences in pain threshold were investigated. It was discovered that this is one of the strongest correlations identified for the personality trait of extraversion. Extraverts were found to have a much higher pain threshold (but they also complained more than introverts during the experiment).
Tolerance for Pain, Extraversion and Neuroticism
R. Lynn and h. J. Eysenck (1961)
University of Exeter University of London

3. Sleep. Various studies have investigated whether there are any significant differences between introverts and extraverts in terms of their need for sleep. One of these studies investigated whether there was any connection between this personality trait and people's most active hours of the day. No significant correlation was discovered.
Individual Differences in Human Circadian Rhythms
James A. Horne, Olov Östberg (1977)

3a. Need for sleep. It's been shown (in several experiments) that introverts and extraverts have different levels of resistance to sleep deprivation. In these situations, introverts function significantly better than extraverts.
Cognitive Performance After Sleep Deprivation: Does Personality Make a Difference?
Daniel J Taylor, Robert M McFatter (2003)

4. Problem solving. Introverts and problem solving. A number of tests have shown that introverts possess greater stamina for problem solving activities. This is one of the more significant differences between these aspects of the personality spectrum.
Personality and Problem Solving
H. J. Eysenck (1959)
Institute of Psychiatry, University of London

5. Stability. The extraversion dimension is stable, and doesn't change much over time. In this study, the test subjects were tested twice, with a four-year interval between testing rounds, and the results from both rounds were compared.
"The Stability of Big-Five Personality Traits"
Cobb-Clark, D.A. & Schurer, S. (2012)
Economics Letters, v.115, p.11

5a. Long-term stability. A longitudinal study followed 163 test subjects over 45 years, and discovered a remarkable stability of personality traits over time.
The Big Five Personality Traits and the Life Course: A 45-Year Longitudinal Study
Stephen Soldz, George E. Vaillant (1999)

6. Differences between the genders. In a Finnish study, 15,000 pairs of twins were tested twice, with a six-year interval between testing rounds. It was found that the personality trait of extraversion didn't seem to be determined by gender, but did exhibit some degree of decline after the age of fifty.
"A Developmental Genetic Analysis of Adult Personality: Extraversion and Neuroticism from 18 to 59 Years of Age"
Viken, Richard J.; Rose, Richard J.; Kaprio, Jaakko; Koskenvuo, Markku (1994)
Journal of Personality and Social Psychology, Vol 66(4), Apr 1994, 722-730

7. Isolation. Introverts have a high tolerance for isolation, and can go without social interaction for a long time (in case anybody needed a scientific study to tell them this).
Introversion and Isolation Tolerance
R. D. Francis (1969)
University College, Wollongong N. S. IV

8. Distractions. This study determined that introverts are more sensitive to noise and unpleasant sounds than extraverts.

"Effects of Noise upon Introverts and Extroverts"

Lionel Standing, Danny Lynn (1990)

Bulletin of the Psychonomic Society, August 1990, Volume 28, Issue 2, pp 138-140

8a. Distractions – noise. Introverts' performance deteriorates more than that of extraverts when they have noise played in their ears.

Musical Preferences and Effects of Music on a Reading Comprehension Test for Extraverts and Introverts (1986)

Leonard Daoussis, and Stuart J. Mckelvie

8b. Distractions – music. This study showed that introverts perform better in silence, and that extraverts perform better with background music.

The Effect of Background Music, Noise and Silence on the Performance of Introvert and Extrovert Students on the Academic Aptitude Test

Sepehrian Azar Firouzeh, Ketabi Afsaneh (2013)

9. Sales. In a study from 1976, the sources of success in sales were investigated. Extraversion was shown to have no significant correlation with success in sales.

Selling and the Salesman: Prediction of Success and Personality Change

Allen A. Turnbull, Jr. (1976)

9a. Stereotypes regarding salespeople. In this study, introvert, ambivert, and extravert salespeople were compared, and despite the stereotype, the group that was found to perform the worst were the extraverts.

Death of a Salesman Stereotype

Melinda Wenner Moyer (2012)

9b. More stereotypes regarding salespeople. In this study of a little over 300 telephone salespeople, it was discovered that the ambivert salespeople were the most successful. Introverts came in second, and extraverts had the least success.

Rethinking the Extraverted Sales Ideal. The Ambivert Advantage

Adam M. Grant (2013)

10. Work environment. I posed a number of questions relating to professional life to groups of introverted, extraverted and ambiverted respondents. The study was performed by questionnaire, and a little over 900 people responded. Among other things, it showed that introverts have a clear preference for shutting the world out.

Blir introverta glada när du ställer in ett möte? (Are Introverts Relieved when you Cancel a Meeting?)

Linus Jonkman (2014)

10a. Work environment – open plan offices. 169 test subjects were asked to work in their own room or in an open plan office. The majority preferred to work in their own room. Introvert test subjects also performed better in more private spaces. The concluding analysis poses a relevant question: is the open plan office beneficial for any organizations?

Performance and Satisfaction in Private versus Nonprivate Work Settings

Lisa K. Block, M.S. (1989)

University of Georgia

11. Inaccurate archetypes. We often have an idea of the kind of personality that is predominant within a specific professional group, and this idea is often incorrect. In this Cuban study, it was shown that most programmers are actually extraverts.

Personality Types of Cuban Software Developers

Daniel Varona, Luiz Fernando Capretz & Yadenis Piñero (2011)

11a. Archetypes about software developers. In this study from 2009, it was made apparent that extraverted programmers produced code more quickly than introverted ones.
The Effect of Personality on Collaborative Task Performance and Interaction
Sinéad Mc Givney, Alan F. Smeaton, Hyowon Lee (2009)

12. Happiness. In one study, comparisons were made between the experiences of happiness of 270 introverted and extraverted people. It was shown that the levels of happiness were the same, but that the activities necessary to achieve them differed between the two groups. Most of all, it was made plain that even though happiness may correlate with extraversion, experienced satisfaction with life is not connected to extraversion, but depends on other factors.
Happiness, Introversion–Extraversion and Happy Introverts
Peter Hills, Michael Argyle (2001)

12a. Happiness and culture. More on happiness. In this study, it was determined that what we refer to as "happiness" isn't a personality trait, but is also (or rather) connected to the culture we live in.
Cultural Constructions of Happiness: Theory and Empirical Evidence
Yukiko Uchida, Vinai Norasakkunkit, Shinobu Kitayama

12b. Happiness and difficult live events. Even though extraversion has often been associated with happiness, a study from 1991 found that introverted prisoners were happier than extraverted ones.
Personality and Life Events as Predictors of Adolescents' Life Satisfaction: Do Life Events Mediate the Link Between Personality and Life Satisfaction?
Man Yee Ho, Fanny M. Cheung, Shu Fai Cheung (1991)

12c. Happiness in the East and in the West. In this study, the happiness of Taiwanese and British test subjects was compared. It was shown that cultural factors made up a large portion of the subjective experience of happiness.

Two Ways to Achieve Happiness: when the East Meets the West

Luo Lu(1999)

12d. Happiness for introverts. In this article, which was published in Psychology Today, author Dan Buettner describes the complexities involved in measuring happiness (as was done in the sources above), and the ways that happiness can differ between different personality types. He also delivers conclusions regarding why introverts score differently on these tests depending on whether they live in the East or in the West.

Are Extroverts Happier Than Introverts?
Insight into Differences Between Two Personality Types
Published on May 14, 2012 by Dan Buettner

12e. Happiness and work satisfaction. 175 office workers were included in this study of experienced work satisfaction. The introverted subset was significantly more satisfied with their tasks and their jobs, while the extraverts felt understimulated.

The Relationship of Extraversion and Neuroticism with Job Preferences and Job Satisfaction for Clerical Employees

Laura Sterns, Ralph A. Alexander, Gerald V. Barrett, and Faye H. Dambrot (1983)

13. Success – academic. This study specifically investigated which personality traits had the strongest correlations with academic success. The answer was introversion.

Personality and Academic Achievement in Three Educational Levels

David s. Goh, and Charles Moore (1978)

13a. Success – artistic. A meta-study of successful art school students was performed in 2006. In it, it's made clear that two traits are strongly correlated with success in the arts: introversion and openness to experience (as defined in the Big Five model, similar to intellectual curiosity).
Preferred Thinking Styles of Professional Fine Artists
Mark C. Gridley, pages 247-248 (2006)

13b. Success – artistic. In a German study from 1973, it was established that two personality traits were clearly dominant in the fifty artistically gifted young people who were included in the sample. They were more introverted, and more neurotic, than the ungifted young artists. Of the gifted group, fifteen were particularly gifted, and among these fifteen, the degree of introversion and neuroticism was even higher than among the rest of the gifted group. A particularly strong correlation between introversion and artistic talent was found in this study.
Introversion-Extraversion and Neuroticism in Gifted and Ungifted Art Students
Karl Otto Götz and Karin Götz
Academy of Fine Arts, Dusseldorf (1973)

14. Boredom. A superpower possessed by introverts is their immunity to boredom. In this study, 25,000 Canadian youths were analyzed, and the conclusion was that extraverts were more likely to find a task boring.
To Produce or not to Produce? Understanding Boredom and the Honor in Underachievement
Lannie Kanevskya & Tacey Keighleybc (2003)

14a. Boredom. This is another article about how introverts can tolerate a larger degree of monotony before deciding that a task is too boring.
Boredom in the Workplace: More than Monotonous Tasks
Lia Loukidou, John Loan-Clarke and Kevin Daniels (2009)

15. Attention. One of a many tests of attention, in which it was shown that introverts are good at achieving focus and keeping it fixed on a single visual stimulus for an extended period of time.

Autonomic Differences Between Extraverts and Introverts During Vigilance

James J. Gange, Russell G. Geen and Stephen G. Harkins (1979)

15a. Focus. Sixty test subjects were asked to focus on a single task for forty minutes. The study supported previous findings indicating that introverts have a greater ability to keep their attention and focus on a particular task.

Personality and Physiological Correlates of Performance Decrement on a Monotonous Task Requiring Sustained Attention

Richard I. Thackray, Karen N. Jones and Robert M. Touchstone (1974)

16. Presence and perception. Although introverts have been shown to maintain focus for longer, extraverts have shown a greater ability to be intensely present in several different studies. They're anchored in the present, and take in more sensory impressions (perceptions) than introverts.

"Orienting of Attention"

Posner, M. I. (1980).

Quarterly Journal of Experimental Psychology, 32, 3-25.

17. Addiction. The connection between personality types and drug abuse has been tested in a number of studies. In this one, the conclusion was that it's the people at the extreme ends of the spectrum (i.e., extreme extraverts and extreme introverts) who are the most prone to becoming drug addicts.

FC18-05 - The Investigation of Relationship Between Personality Types (Introvert - Extravert) and People's Tendency to Narcotics Addiction

H. Ghorbani Amiri, T. Ahmadi Gatab (2011)

17a. Addiction – nicotine. In this study of smokers, it was shown that there were no significant differences between people who took up smoking in terms of personality traits. However, the introverts tend to have an easier time giving it up.
Introverts Give up Smoking More Often than Extraverts
Ásgeir R. Helgason, Mats Fredrikson, Tadeusz Dyba, Gunnar Steineck (1995)

18. Time estimation. Introverts experience time more accurately than extraverts. In this study, the test subjects wore blindfolds, and were asked to estimate when fifteen minutes had passed. Extraverted test subjects had a much larger margin of error than introverted test subjects.
Personality and Time Estimation in Sensory Deprivation
G. F. Reed and j. C. Kenna, University of Manchester (1967)

19. The Internet and introversion. In a study of behavior in online chats, it was revealed that introverts generally feel that they're able to be themselves when they communicate through text online, while extraverts feel that their true selves shine through in actual physical encounters.
"'On the Internet No One Knows I'm an Introvert': Extroversion, Neuroticism, and Internet Interaction"
Yair Amichai-Hamburger, Galit Wainapel, and Shaul Fox.
CyberPsychology & Behavior (2002).

19a. Internet addiction. This study investigated which personality traits are predictive of Internet addiction. Extraversion-Introversion was included in the study, but no correlation was found. Instead, gaming addiction seems to be related to impulse control issues.
"Extraversion, Impulsivity, and Online Group Membership as Predictors of Problematic Internet Use"
Andrew J. Mottram and Michele J. Fleming
CyberPsychology & Behavior, June 2009, 12(3): 319-321.

20. IQ. Introverts and extraverts don't seem to differ significantly in terms of IQ.

A Study of the Relation Between IQ and Personality Types Among Male and Female Students of Tabriz

Vafaiee B., Dadashzadeh H. (2004)

20a. IQ. Another study that attempted to match specific personality traits with IQ scores. Again, no clear correlation was found.

"The Relationships Between Introversion-Extraversion, Neuroticism and Performance in School Examinations"

Dennis child (1964)

British Journal of Educational Psychology, Volume 34, Issue 2, pages 187–196, June (1964)

21. Reaction times. In this Romanian study, reaction time and choice of action were measured in a test involving both introverted and extraverted test subjects. Two differences were discovered: Extraverts reacted significantly faster, but introverts made significantly better choices.

Significant Differences Between Introvert and Extrovert People's Simple Reaction Time in Conflict Situations

Vlad Burtăverde, Teodor Mihăilă, University of Bucharest, Department of Psychology (2011)

22. Gifted children. This study from 1966 investigated the characteristics common to children who were moved up a grade in school. Introversion was a significant and distinctive feature of this group.

"Personality and Social Status"

Dennis Child (1966)

British Journal of Social and Clinical Psychology, Volume 5, Issue 3, pages 196–199, September 1966

23. Memory. In a study from 1979, the memories of forty students were tested. The introverted subset of the test subjects proved to retain more lasting and visual memories of a task. This supported the hypothesis that introverts are better at visualizing their thoughts, which strengthened their long-term memory of the task.

"Introversion–Extraversion and Mental Imagery"
Gralton, Moira A.; Hayes, Yvonne A.; Richardson, John T.
Journal of Mental Imagery, Vol 3(1-2), 1979

23a. Working memory. In a study from the year 2000, the working memories of introverted and extraverted test subjects were measured. It was found that extraverts are faster at connecting their working memories (short-term memory) to particular situations. They're more anchored in the present.

"Introversion and Working Memory: Central Executive Differences"
Matthew D Lieberman (2000)
Personality and Individual Differences, Vol 28(3), Mar 2000, 479-486

24. Multitasking. 160 students were included in this study, in which 12 different varieties of multitasking were tested. Their results here were compared to their personality types and their attitudes to multitasking. The most important conclusion drawn from this study was that none of the personality types performed significantly better than the others when multitasking. However, extraverts displayed a strong tendency to prefer a multitasking approach to work.

Predicting Multitasking Performance and Understanding the Nomological Network of Polychronicity
Girgis, Zackary Magdy (2010)

24a. Successful multitasking. Because of the preceding study, a closer look at the concept of multitasking would be of interest. In a study from 2005, it was found that the most important factors for successful multitasking are attention and working memory.

"Working Memory, Fluid Intelligence, and Attention Are Predictors of Multitasking Performance, but Polychronicity and Extraversion Are Not"

Cornelius J. Konig, Markus Buhner & Gesine Murling

Human Performance, Volume 18, Issue 3, 2005(2005), pages 243-266

25. Risk taking. This article describes various studies of risk taking and the personality traits that are connected to them. The trait that is most clearly connected to unmotivated risk taking is extraversion.

Personality and domain-specific risk taking

Nigel Nicholson Corresponding author, Emma Soane, Mark Fenton-O'Creevy & Paul Willman (2005)

25a. Risk taking in groups. Risk taking personalities with a high degree of extraversion also tend to greatly influence and dominate decision processes in groups.

"Personality and Group Decisions Involving Risk"

Rim, Y.

The Psychological Record, Vol 14(1), 37-45 (1964)

25b. Risk taking in groups – the military. The US army's analysis of personalities concluded that a group needs a balance between different personality traits to be able to make correct decisions. Diversity of personality traits mitigates the negative phenomenon of groupthink.

Integrating Staff Elements, Personality Type and Groupthink

Walch, Ronald D. (2009)

25c. Genes and risk taking. This article indicates which genes influence dopamine rushes and risk-taking behavior.

Genetic Determinants of Financial Risk Taking

Camelia M. Kuhnen, Joan Y. Chiao (2009)

25d. Risk taking in traffic. A study examined how a sample of about 1,000 male students behaved in traffic. The extraverted group caused accidents with a significantly higher frequency. (Which means that you should always let the introvert drive).
Introversion-extraversion and motor vehicle driver behavior
Bernard J. Fine (1963)

25e. Optimism and risk taking. Risk taking is thought to be connected to optimism. This interesting study confirmed that extraversion and optimism are connected. However, there was no connection between pessimism and introversion. Instead, pessimism was connected to the personality trait of neuroticism. This is interesting, because the general conception is that pessimism is simply the absence of optimism.
"Distinguishing Optimism from Pessimism: Relations to Fundamental Dimensions of Mood and Personality"
Marshall, Grant N.; Wortman, Camille B.; Kusulas, Jeffrey W.; Hervig, Linda K.; Vickers Jr., Ross R.
Journal of Personality and Social Psychology, Vol 62(6), 1067-1074 Jun (1992)

26. Heredity. Hans Eysenck tested the personalities of fifty-six pairs of twins. His study concluded that identical twins' personalities are more alike than those of fraternal twins. This was one of the first studies to suggest that personality has a biological component, which is hereditary in nature.
The Inheritance of Extraversion-Introversion
H.J. Eysenck (1956)

26a. Heredity. A study of 1,200 Australian twins connected personality traits to specific genes. The strongest hereditary connection discovered was between extraversion and neuroticism

A Genome-Wide Scan for Eysenckian Personality Dimensions in Adolescent Twin Sibships: Psychoticism, Extraversion, Neuroticism, and Lie

Nathan A. Gillespie, Gu Zhu, David M. Evans, Sarah E. Medland, Margie J. Wright and Nick G. Martin (2008)

27. Leadership. This study investigated how extraverted leadership works in practice. The conclusion was that a leader with a high degree of extraversion performs well in situations where the work force is passive, while leaders whose personalities are more introverted perform better with more pro-active and independent workforces.

Reversing the Extraverted Leadership Advantage: The Role of Employee Proactivity

Adam M. Grant, Francesca Gino, and David A. Hofmann (2011)

27a. Introverted leadership. In 2010, the Harvard Business School published an article that was based on a number of different studies of leadership. In it, they showed that introverted leaders are an especially good fit for independent and proactive co-workers. Among the advantages of introverted leaders that were mentioned was the fact that they don't monopolize meetings.

Introverts: The Best Leaders for Proactive Employees

Carmen Nobel (2010)

28. Performance. In a Romanian study from 2007, 247 students were asked to perform in different circumstances. It was established that extraverts performed the best in competition-like situations, while introverts performed the best when there were no competitive elements involved. By the way, this aligns nicely with Hans Eysenck's theories.

The Influence of Extraversion on the Performances in Cooperative and Competitive Activities
Cristina - Corina ŞTIR, University of Galaţi No. 47, Romania (2007)

28a. Group performance. In a study, eight-two work teams were compared. Some of the teams were homogenous in terms of the members' personalities, and other teams were more mixed. These teams were compared according to the Big Five model. It turned out that certain traits improve the team's performance when it is homogenous (e.g., conscientiousness). However, there was a clear indication that a spread of introversion-extraversion among a team's members was beneficial in terms of performance. In this respect, the study revealed that teams ought to have both introverts and extraverts among their members.

The Relationship between Work-Team Personality Composition and the Job Performance of Teams
George A. Neuman. Northern Illinois University (1999)

29. Punishment. This study, which was performed in 1937, would have been considered ethically dubious by today's standards. In it, the reactions of introverted and extraverted students to criticism and blame were tested. The conclusion was that introverts react stronger to criticism, and therefore change their performance to a higher degree than extraverts in response to it.

"The Effect of Repeated Praise or Blame on the Performance of Introverts and Extroverts"
Forlano, G.; Axelrod, H. C.
Journal of Educational Psychology, Vol 28 (1937)

30. Professional success. In a study of the concept of talent, it was shown that extraversion is a most relevant dimension, but that it's effects also depend on the presence of another personality trait; conscientiousness. A person who has a high level of both of these traits will often be highly prized at his or her workplace. However, if it's combined with low conscientiousness, high extraversion will significantly devalue this estimation.

The Interactive Effects of Extraversion and Conscientiousness on Performance

L. A. Witt (2002)

30a. Professional success and personality. Just over 200 warehouse workers were compared. Their personalities were connected with their levels of proficiency at their jobs. There was only a very weak correlation between personality traits and skill levels.

Cognitive Ability as a Moderator of the Relationship Between Personality and Job Performance

Patrick M. Wright, K. Michele Kacmar, Gary C. McMahan and Kevin Deleeuw (1995)

31. On speakers. In this study, extravert and introvert speakers were compared. Among other things, it was made plain that extraverts are more likely to go over their allotted speaking time, and also use a greater number of irrelevant words.

A Study of Personality Traits of Mature Actors and Mature Public Speakers

Elwood Murray & James A. Tracy (1935)

32. Tone of voice. In this study, personality traits were investigated in relation to preferred speech volume. Introverts were found to prefer to speak more silently than extraverts.

A Possible Basis for the Association of Voice Characteristics and Personality Traits

Edith B. Mallory & Virginia R. Miller (1958)

33. Shyness. This study attempted to define what shyness is. It was determined that shyness and introversion are not the same thing. Shyness appears to be a completely separate trait.

Shyness as a Dimension of Personality
W. R. Crazier*. (2011)

34. Blood pressure. In a Japanese study, it was found that there tends to be a difference in the same patient's blood pressure, depending on whether it's measured at home or at the hospital. Among introverts, this difference was significant, which suggests that they're more sensitive to circumstances.

Introversion Associated with Large Differences Between Screening Blood Pressure and Home Blood Pressure Measurement: the Ohasama Study
Hozawa, Atsushi; Ohkubo, Takayoshi; Obara, Taku; Metoki, Hirohito; Kikuya, Masahiro; Asayama, Kei; Totsune, Kazuhito; Hashimoto, Junichiro; Hoshi, Haruhisa; Arai, Yumiko; Satoh, Hiroshi; Hosokawa, Toru; Imai, Yutaka (2006)

35. Thought processes. The differences between introverts' and extraverts' thought processes have been examined in various studies. In this one, electrode scanning revealed that introverts and extraverts display significantly different brain activity when their eyes are closed.

Extraversion—Introversion and the EEG
Anthony Gale, Michael Coles and Jennifer Blaydon (1969)

35a. Thought processes. Another study using electrodes revealed clear differences between extraverted and introverted subjects, particularly in the frontal lobes.

"Computerized EEG and Personality"
Ramírez Pérez A, Martínez López-Coterilla M, Fajardo López A, Lardelli Claret A
Actas Luso-espanolas de Neurologia, Psiquiatria y Ciencias Afines, (1989)

278

35b. Thought processes and monotony. Brain activity was measured when extremely introverted and extremely extraverted test subjects were asked to perform a monotonous task for forty minutes. The introverts managed to produce better results in performing the task, with less experienced exertion.

Energetical Bases of Extraversion: Effort, Arousal, EEG, and Performance

André Beauducela, Burkhard Brockeb, Anja Leuec (2006)

35c. Social thought processes. Introvert people's brains are more strongly activated by facial expressions than by brain teasers. The social dimension of life is thought to have a more intense effect on an introverted person.

Event-Related Desynchronization in the EEG During Emotional and Cognitive Information Processing: Differential Effects of Extraversion

Andreas Fink (2005)

35d. Thought processes – brain waves. In this study, alpha waves in the brain were examined. It turned out that extraverts were more active in this sense (or, to be more precise, they had a higher amplitude). Alpha waves are thought to be related to visual impressions and perception, or, to put it more simply, to one's degree of presence in the here and now.

Personality and Male-Female Influences on the EEG Alpha Rhythm

J.F.W. Deakin , K.A. Exley (1979)

35e. Thought processes – blood flow. Brain blood flow differs between introverted and extraverted test subjects. It seems that introverts have a stronger preference for using their frontal lobes than extraverts.

"Regional Patterns of Cortical Blood Flow Distinguish Extraverts from Introverts"

G. Stenberg, J. Risberg, S. Warkentin, I. Rosén (1990)

Personality and Individual Differences Volume 11, Issue 7, 663–673

36. ADHD. In a French study performed on children with ADHD, it was observed that the children included in the study were more extraverted than the average for the population. A number of studies have investigated the diagnosis of ADHD, and extraversion has been suggested to be a major component many times (when the Big Five has been used as a tool, it's often been combined with low conscientiousness)

A Study of Temperament and Personality in Children Diagnosed with Attention-Deficit Hyperactivity Disorder (ADHD)

Bouvard M, Sigel L, Laurent A

Laboratoire LIP, université de Savoie, BP 1104, 73011 Chambéry cedex, (2012)

37. Asperger syndrome. In an American study, twenty individuals who had been diagnosed with Asperger syndrome were analyzed. They were found to be twenty-five to thirty-five percent more introverted than the average for the population. For this reason, there are some psychologists who claim that introversion can be thought of as a mild form of autism.

MMPI-2 Personality Profiles of High-Functioning Adults with Autism Spectrum Disorders

Sally Ozonoff, University of California (2006)

38. Cultural differences. A study compared different cultures with a set of parameters that are thought to indicate extraversion or introversion on the national level. Among other things, the study determined that the US is the most extraverted country in the world, and that Japan is the most introverted.

National Differences in Extraversion and Neuroticism

R. Lynn and s. L. Hampson (1975)

38a. Cultural differences – the Big Five. In another study, the distribution of the Big Five personality traits in fifty-six different countries was investigated. In this study, Japan and Bangladesh were named the least extraverted nations in the world.

The Geographic Distribution of Big Five Personality Traits: Patterns and Profiles of Human Self-Description Across 56 Nations

David P. Schmitt, Jüri Allik, Robert R. McCrae and Verónica Benet-Martínez (2007)

39. Global population. An estimate based on the Myers-Briggs test database has determined that twenty-five to thirty percent of the US population are introverts. It's worth knowing that other estimates vary from twenty to fifty-two percent, depending on the source of the information.

Myers-Briggs Type Indicator, A/B Personality Types, and Locus of Control: Where Do They Intersect?

Cherie E. Fretwell, Carmen C. Lewis, Maureen Hannay, Troy University (2013)

39a. Proportion of introverts – gender. In 1998, Myers-Briggs made an estimate, and arrived at the conclusion that on average, women in the US were three percent more extraverted than men.

MBTI Manual: A Guide to the Development and Use of the Myers-Briggs Type Indicator (3rd ed.)

Myers, I. B., McCaulley, M. H., Quenk, N. L., & Hammer, A. L. (1998). Palo Alto.

39b. Proportion of introverts – trends. A study of national extraversion confirmed that the world (in the West) had become more and more extraverted since the 1950s.

Fluctuations in National Levels of Neuroticism and Extraversion, 1935–1970

R. Lynn and S. L. Hampson (2011)

39c. Generations. In a longitudinal study, the personality traits of 1.4 million Americans, who have been responding to questionnaires since the 1930s, were compared. The results reveal that millennials have the highest recorded self-esteem and stress levels since the study began.

Generational Differences in Psychological Traits and Their Impact on the Workplace

Jean M. Twenge, Department of Psychology, San Diego State University. Stacy M. Campbell (2008)

39d. Generations. In this meta-study, which included just over 16,000 American young adults, changes in personality traits over several decades (between 1966 and 1993) were analyzed. It was evident that extraversion had increased significantly in that time frame.

Birth Cohort Changes in Extraversion: a Cross-Temporal Meta-Analysis

Jean M. Twenge (2001)

39e. Proportion of introverts – emigrants. A study from 2006 examined how islanders differ from the mainland populations. It also studied differences between emigrants and people who had remained in a single geographic location for many generations. It turned out that emigrants are significantly more extraverted than the other groups.

The Adaptive Value of Personality Differences Revealed by Small Island Population Dynamics

Andrea S. Camperio Ciani, Claudio Capiluppi, Antonio Veronese and Giuseppe Sartori (2006)

40. Status – fashion interest. This word describes our perceived social standing in relation to others. Some of the phenomena associated with status are physical appearance, fashion, titles, and material wealth. Common to several studies is the claim that extraverts attach more importance to status than introverts. This is most likely due to the fact that this is a social currency. This study from 2012 analyzed the things that characterize people who are interested in fashion. The primary trait they shared was extraversion.

Fashion Enthusiasts

Casey Finigan, University of Massachusetts Boston (2012)

40a. Status – plastic surgery. 155 patients who had all recently undergone plastic surgery were compared with the general population. It turned out that they were more extraverted prior to the surgery, but it was also shown that their extraverted features were strengthened after this.

Cosmetic Surgery and the Relationship Between Appearance Satisfaction and Extraversion: Testing a Transactional Model of Personality

Tilmann von Soest, Ingela L. Kvalema, Knut C. Skolleborg, Helge E. Roald (2009)

41. Gossip. This rather unusual study investigated how introverts and extraverts relate to gossip. The conclusion was that both groups have approximately the same knowledge of celebrity gossip, but that introverts are less likely to use it as a conversation piece.

"Gossip and the Introvert"

Davis, F. B.; Rulon, P. J.

The Journal of Abnormal and Social Psychology, Vol 30(1), Apr (1935)

42. Lies. In a study where fake job interviews were organized, it became apparent that the greater the degree of extraversion possessed by the jobseeker was, the more likely this person was to lie to get the job.

Looking Good and Lying to Do It: Deception as an Impression Management Strategy in Job Interviews

Brent Weiss and Robert S. Feldman (2006)

43. Empathy. Although the opposite might seem the more reasonable assumption, introverts are generally more empathic than extraverts. Introverts who also possess a high degree of neuroticism are particularly empathic according to a study from 1974.

"Correlates of Emotional Empathy"

Rim, Y

Scientia Paedagogica Experimentalis, Vol 11(2), 1974, 197-202.

44. Communications styles. Introverts and extraverts prefer to use different kinds of words. One of the conclusions drawn in the study was that it's somewhat easier to have confidence in what introverts communicate, because it's based on fact to a greater degree.

Extraverted People Talk More Abstractly, Introverts Are More Concrete

Camiel J. Beukeboom, Martin Tanis, Ivar E. Vermeulen (2012)

45. Learning styles. A study from 1992 investigated the impact of personality traits on people's learning styles. The study claimed that the extraversion-introversion dimension has an especially large impact.

Personality and Learning Style: A Study of Three Instruments

Adrian Furnham (1992)

45a. Learning styles. Two hundred telephone salespeople were included in a study of learning styles. During the study, it was revealed that extraversion-introversion plays a great role in the preferred learning style of each individual.

Personality, Learning Style and Work Performance
Adrian Furnham, Chris J Jackson, Tony Miller (1999)

45b. Learning styles – memory skills. In this study, a comparison was made of introverted and extraverted twelve-year-olds' abilities to remember information. There was a significant difference in their abilities. Introverts were better at remembering image-based content, while extraverts were better at remembering what was said, or verbal content.

The Relationship Between Extraversion and Verbal-Imagery Learning style in Twelve-Year-Old Children
R.J. Riding, V.A. Dyer (1980)

46. Falsification. Acting as another personality type than your own for extended periods of time is called "falsification of type". In her research, Dr. Katherine Benziger has arrived at the conclusion that this behavior is extremely strenuous for the brain. She thinks it's a strong contributing factor in cases of burnout.

Falsification of Type
Katherine Benziger (1995)

47. Narcissism. Narcissism denotes an unhealthy degree of self-centeredness. It's self-infatuation coupled with grandiose overestimations of one's own abilities. In a study of the personality traits associated with narcissism, extraversion was strongly correlated.

The Narcissistic Personality Inventory: Alternative Form Reliability and Further Evidence of Construct Validity
Robert Raskin & Calvin S. Hall (1981)

47a. Narcissism and Facebook. A recent study investigated the characteristic traits of a Facebook user. It was shown that Facebook's users were more extraverted and narcissistic than the average person. They also generally experienced less social interaction than people who don't use Facebook. It's worth noting that the study was performed before Facebook became as extremely widespread as it is today.

Who Uses Facebook? An Investigation into the Relationship Between the Big Five, Shyness, Narcissism, Loneliness, and Facebook Usage
Tracii Ryan, Sophia Xenos (2011)

48. Self-esteem. Several studies have been done on the subject of self-esteem. In most cases, extraversion correlates positively with high self-esteem. In a meta-study, age, gender, ethnicity and personality traits were all compared. The most robust correlation was that between extraversion and self-esteem.

Personality Correlates of Self-Esteem
Richard W. Robins, Jessica L. Tracy, Kali Trzesniewski, Jeff Potter, Samuel D. Gosling (2001)

49. Partnership. There have been four decades of debate over whether we look for somebody like ourselves, or somebody who has the things we don't have. There have been studies made that have looked closer at the personality aspect of this. In a study from 1997, it turned out that people are happier in relationships with people who have the opposite traits. That is to say, if you're passive, you'll tend to be more comfortable in relationships with people who are more dominant.

"When Do Opposites Attract? Interpersonal Complementarity Versus Similarity"
Dryer, D. Christopher; Horowitz, Leonard M.
Journal of Personality and Social Psychology, Vol 72(3), 592-603. Mar (1997)

49a. Partnership – list of requirements. In a Dutch study, the question of what people consciously seek in a life partner was investigated. The most common response was that we seek somebody who complements us rather than somebody who is like us.

Do People Know What They Want: A Similar or Complementary Partner?

Pieternel Dijkstra, Department of Psychology, University of Groningen (2008)

50. Infidelity. 470 people took part in this study on infidelity. There were three things that significantly influenced somebody's propensity to be unfaithful. These were: sexual confidence, forgiving attitude to infidelity, and the personality trait of extraversion.

"A Semi-model of Predictive Factors for Mixed Infidelity"

Scutaru, Elena Laura; Turliuc, Maria-Nicoleta

AAICUPS, Volume 2013; 22(2): 35–51 (2013)

51. Group dynamics. Do groups become more tightly knit when their members resemble one another? In the case of extraversion, the answer is no. Studies have shown that the relation is the opposite. If a group is mainly extraverted, its cohesion will be strengthened by the addition of an introvert. And the reverse is also true.

When Opposites Attract: A Multi-Sample Demonstration of Complementary Person-Team Fit on Extraversion

Amy Kristof-Brown, Murray R. Barrick and Cynthia Kay Stevens (2005)

52. The military. There are countless studies that explore how introverts function in the military. A NATO study on preferable personality traits for military personnel suggested that introverted soldiers are more useful in sensitive areas, because they have been proven to be less disposed to react aggressively in stressful situations.

Modeling Cultural Behavior for Military Virtual Training

Philip Kerbusch, Jeffrey Schram, Karel van den Bosch (2011)

52a. The military. 193 officers were analyzed using the Myers-Briggs Type Indicator test. It was discovered that all traits were represented, and that there was an interplay between introverts and extraverts that was extremely valuable in military operations.

Frequencies of Myers Briggs Type Indicator (MBTI) Among Military Leaders
Dianna Lea Williams 1999

52b. The military – officer profiling. An Australian study examined one hundred officers using the Big Five model. It was found that the most characteristic trait of effective leaders was low extraversion and high conscientiousness.

"The Role of Personality in Leadership: An Application of the Five-Factor Model in the Australian Military"
McCormack, Luke; Mellor, David
Military Psychology, Vol 14(3), 2002, 179-197

53. Personal space. Introverts and extraverts seem to have the same preference in terms of the size of their personal space. However, introverts react more strongly to invasions of their personal space.

"Personal Space and its Relation to Extraversion-Introversion"
Williams, John L,
Canadian Journal of Behavioural Science, Vol 3(2), Apr 1971, 156-160.

54. The tension surrounding the word *introvert*. Something that I've noticed while reading hundreds of studies of introversion, is how charged with value this word seems to be. In older studies, from the '30s, '40s, and '50s, introverted traits were described as noble and desirable (for instance, "introverts gossip less than extraverts". In more recent studies, the trait is much more problematized (happiness has actually come to be described as the trait of extraversion in the last few years). Introversion has almost become a diagnosis. This aspect of Western culture is hard to ignore. Since my book was written, a thesis that's worth taking a look at has been published on this matter. It describes how introversion went from being an ideal, to being a norm, and then became a pathological state.

Amidst a Culture of Noise Silence is Still Golden: a Sociocultural Historical Analysis of the Pathologization of Introversion

Fudjack, Sara L.

54a. Normal or pathological? *Psychology Today* published an article about how, in 2010, the American Psychology Association wanted to introduce the diagnosis Introversion into the DMS-5 (which is a manual of psychological diagnosis criteria). After much debate, it was retracted.

Are Introverts Nuts? Is There Something Wrong with you if you're an Introvert?

Nancy Ancowitz (2010)

55. Famous people who are introverts? Barack Obama. The claims regarding Barack's introversion originally come from his own memoirs, where he gives a detailed account of his approach to life and his world-view. Many other sources, including Susan Cain and political commentator Matt Lewis, have backed the claims that he's an introvert.

The 2012 Campaign: A Tale of Two Introverts?

MATT LEWIS (2012) *DailyCaller*

34167668R00163

Made in the USA
San Bernardino, CA
20 May 2016